Tying the Knot

Other Books by Jade River

The Cella Training Program Workbook

The Cella Training Program: A course of Study for
Women Witches

To Know: A Guide to Women's Magic and Spirituality

How to Incorporate a Non-Profit Religious Organization

Tying the Knot

A Gender-Neutral Guide
to Handfastings or Weddings
for Pagans and Goddess Worshipers

by

Jade River

Tying the Knot: A Gender-Neutral Guide to
Handfastings or Weddings for Pagans and Goddess Worshippers,
Second Edition by Jade River.
Copyright © 2004 Samantha Jade River. All rights reserved.

Editing by Daña Alder, and
Certain book design by Eva Bee, and
Cover design elements by Kassandra Sojourner.
Copyright © 2004 *Creatrix Resource Library LLC*. All rights reserved.

ISBN Number: 0-9760604-2-6

Published by *Creatrix Resource Library LLC*,
a *Creatrix Books LLC* company

Creatrix

P.O. Box 366
Cottage Grove, WI 53527

Printed in the USA.

To my son Casey,

On the occasion of his wedding

Acknowledgements

My thanks to:

All the couples who have allowed me to learn about handfastings
by Priestessing theirs.

Kathryn Ponzer and Emmie Harrison for allowing me to use their
handfasting ceremony, "A Handfasting Ceremony for Couples
Wishing to Acknowledge their Children",
as an example in this book.

Daña Alder for her invaluable assistance with editing.

Laura Varela and Megan Webster for their expert Proofreading.

The women of the Re-formed Congregation of the Goddess
who are always an inspiration.

And finally, my heartfelt thanks to my partner, Kevyn,
for her love and support.

Contents

Appendices

Introduction

Paganism is reported to be the fastest growing religion in North America. As the Craft continues to grow, we have drawn from the European roots of the Craft and begun creating traditions that have meaning to us as we enter a new era. In conventional North American culture, there are few rites of passage to mark like transitions. As a whole, our culture has no coming of age, birth, menarche, or croning rituals.

There are however, some observances that have retained a place in culture. One of the most common of these is the "wedding." It is not surprising that many of us have preconceived notions of what is appropriate for a wedding. Among many Pagans, weddings are called handfastings. This book contains examples and options for handfastings. It includes both traditional and non-traditional choices. It incorporated information for those joining with people of the same or opposite sex. You are free to pick and choose among the alternatives, modeling a ceremony to fit your needs, beliefs, and interests. Any activity you feel is inappropriate should not have a place in your ritual.

Your handfasting is a time for you and your future partner to create a rite that will be meaningful to you both. It is a way to seal your live with the magical energy of your friends and family. It is also a time for you to declare your intention to be recognized as partners by your community. What is significant to each of you and how you incorporate these activities into ceremony are highly personal decisions. This book explores many of the choices available as options for a handfasting. If you have a specific ritual idea, but don't find it included in this text, it does not mean you shouldn't consider it. Make your ceremony something meaningful and magical for both of you. Planning and intention can help you create a handfasting you can look back on with pleasure and pride.

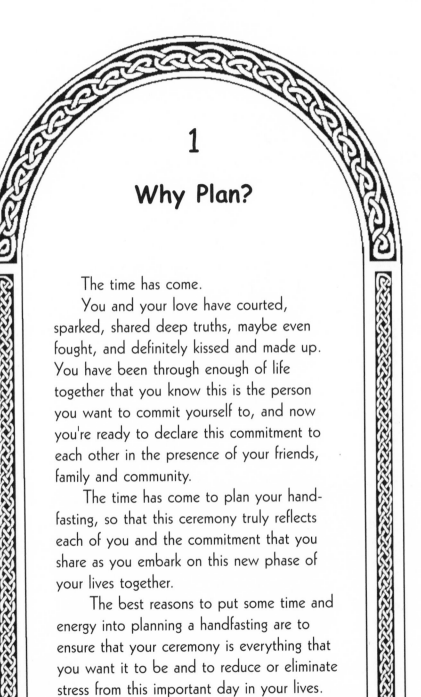

1

Why Plan?

The time has come.

You and your love have courted, sparked, shared deep truths, maybe even fought, and definitely kissed and made up. You have been through enough of life together that you know this is the person you want to commit yourself to, and now you're ready to declare this commitment to each other in the presence of your friends, family and community.

The time has come to plan your handfasting, so that this ceremony truly reflects each of you and the commitment that you share as you embark on this new phase of your lives together.

The best reasons to put some time and energy into planning a handfasting are to ensure that your ceremony is everything that you want it to be and to reduce or eliminate stress from this important day in your lives. You may find that the magic of your handfasting ceremony is enhanced if you're not worrying about the many details involved.

A handfasting is a magical act best done with reflection and forethought. While it's true that some couples decide impulsively to be handfasted or trysted at a festival or other gathering, and the spontaneity of these ceremonies can be fun and refreshing, most couples in these situations have had little opportunity in the moment to consider the deep magical significance of this act.

Ideally, preparation for a handfasting includes both arranging the logistical details and defining your magical intention, with both partners spending time visioning, imagining, discussing and coming together to create a shared idea of the commitment they are making, as well as how their commitment can best be honored and sanctified. Most people require some time to imagine and conceptualize fully a magical bond. Taking the time to clarify the intent of your ceremony and your pledge can enrich both.

Many Craft traditions have a concept wherein the participants define together the intention of the magic to be performed before any magical work begins. The basic steps are:

◆ Developing a shared vision of the language and feeling of the magical intention through discussion, imaging and reflection.

◆ Statements by each group member, sharing her/his concept of the goal of the magic.

◆ If there are differences, seeking clarification until all members can articulate, demonstrate and share the same intention.

◆ Being sure that all members agree about the intent of the magic before joining their energy to create it.

Magical planning for a handfasting requires no less intention. There are questions to be answered, decisions to be made and goals to be clarified. Interestingly, some people will not participate in a spell to heal the earth without a specific discussion of the intent but will be handfasted with little shared awareness of the purpose and direction of the ceremony.

Unless there is a compelling reason to do otherwise, take your time envisioning your future. It is the most precious joining gift you can give yourself and your loved one. The clearer each one of you is about the meaning of your handfasting, the richer the magic will be.

Although it is possible to plan a handfasting in a few weeks, it is generally easier to organize the activities, magic and participants with several months or even a year of lead-time.

Many couples rely heavily on the support of family and friends to help plan and attend to the details that comprise their ceremony. Your knowledge of the views and attitudes held by these people toward Paganism may be a good guide for whether or not they will be inclined to help.

They may be hesitant or unwilling to participate in a ritual based on the Craft, and even when family and friends are support-ive, they may be unfamiliar with the purpose and traditions involved. It will be best if you have the assistance of Craft-know-ledgeable people for planning. You may want to ask those in your grove, circle, nest or coven to help you with plan-ning and decision-making.

Whether you envision a large or a small event, you may feel overwhelmed or at least anxious for a variety of reasons at the idea of planning a handfasting. There is often pressure for the ceremony and any accompanying celebration to be perfect. Although almost all of the best handfasting stories are based on things that have gone "wrong," the expectation for an ideal event can loom large.

Emotional preparation for the ritual can also cause apprehension.

A handfasting changes your life. Making a commitment with another to share your lives is the beginning of a new life-phase for both of you. Many people are disturbed by change. Even though you may truly and deeply want to pledge your life to your future partner, this does not guarantee you will never feel uncertain during the process. Making a commitment to another person, being the focus of magical work and planning one of the biggest parties of your life may all conspire to cause doubts.

No matter what the source of your apprehension, planning can help. Knowing what is supposed to happen can dispel uncertainty and bring a broader perspective. Planning an event of this nature can be so complicated that there is an entire profession — wedding consultants — devoted to lifting these responsibilities from the shoulders of the couple. If you feel overwhelmed or anxious, developing a plan to address your concerns is probably the best antidote.

This guide is intended to answer your questions and give you ideas to plan a handfasting that reflects the magic of your love and your bond to one another.

2

The Purpose

A Public Declaration: Why Do It?

Love is a blessing and a gift, something we search for and value. Standing in front of your friends and family to announce that you are committing yourself to another person is a time-honored and valued tradition in many cultures. It is the way we show our community, relatives and friends that we consider our relationship to be genuine and lasting. By making a public declaration, we ask our family and friends to join us in maintaining that bond.

In Western culture, having a public ceremony conveys that we are serious about our partner and our relationship to them sends a signal with many levels of meaning. It communicates that you and your partner consider yourselves a couple. It notifies your family and friends that you intend to build a life together, and it announces the formal beginning of that life. A public commitment communicates that your relationship has changed: You would like to spend the foreseeable future with this individual and you invite others to acknowledge and celebrate this intention with you.

While the right to make a commitment that is recognized under the law has been available to heterosexual couples for centuries, only recently have state marriage licenses been issued to lesbians and gay men, who have worked hard with their allies for this civil right. Legal breakthroughs in the Netherlands, Canada and Massachusetts and evolutionary changes in mainstream views about lesbian and gay marriage indicate that the commitment ceremonies which same-sex couples have celebrated for many years may be joined by more widespread legal recognition in the future.

This book is intended to guide the planning for a handfasting between same-sex couples or different-sex couples, whether the ceremony will involve a state-issued marriage license or not.

Commitment

A handfasting creates a magical bond that commits two partners to each other. Before moving very far into the planning process, set aside some time to discuss the nature of your commitment with your partner-to-be. The word "commitment" means different things to different people. Will your pledge be the same as that in a conventional marriage? If you are a heterosexual couple (or a lesbian/gay couple in select locations), do you wish to formalize your union with a marriage license? Will you promise sexual fidelity? Is your commitment for a lifetime?

It is important to discuss and reach agreement on these and many other subjects regarding the nature of your commitment. There are no right answers. It is simply prudent to be sure that you and your partner-to-be agree. Your answers affect the specific vows that you make and even the way magic is used during your ceremony. Having an understanding of the boundaries of your commitment can alleviate later conflicts and make planning proceed more smoothly.

Don't be concerned if your answers to these questions are not traditional, as alternative concepts and creative ideas can be incorporated easily into a handfasting. For instance, some couples make their commitment for a year-and-a-day with the option to renegotiate their pledge at the end of that time. Some people commit to having an open relationship or include a polyamorous pledge (acknowledging that they each may love more than one person at a time). Still others prefer to create a bond that includes more than two people. The critical factor is that all partners agree on the boundaries of the commitment, but otherwise there is no need to be limited by established customs.

If you want to make an alternative type of commitment, discuss this with the Priest/ess who will perform your ceremony. Although this happens rarely, s/he may not be willing to perform an unconventional ritual. More likely, your Priest/ess will want to discuss how your choices can be incorporated into the ritual. S/he may want to review the standard handfasting liturgy with you and make changes that reflect your wishes.

◆ As you begin to plan your handfasting and discuss these issues with your partner and others, remember to stay in touch with your own feelings. If you feel discomfort about being handfasted, it is wise to explore the reasons for your "cold feet." If doubt threatens to overwhelm you, consider re-thinking whether this is the right time, place or person for you to make a commitment.

◆ Some people fear commitment; to them, it equals confinement. If your uncertainty is from this source, you may want to talk with a trusted friend, counselor or Priest/ess. It is not advisable to make a pledge when you have serious doubts. Regardless of whether your doubts are about you or your partner-to-be, the time to resolve them is before your ceremony, not during or after.

Too much certainty can also be unwise. I once attended a hand-fasting where the couple promised to honor their commitment "in this life and the next." No matter how much you love someone, obligating yourself magically for more than your current lifetime is not wise. Entering a new life already magically bound to another person could be a blessing or it could be a burden. For most of us, the forms and circumstances of our future lives are a mystery. Our ability to keep a pledge from one life to another depends on coming into the other life with certainty that we would have access to the psychic skills needed to remember and act on the pledge, not to mention that binding oneself between lives can compromise the choices available to us for a particular life

On a very practical level, in this life the magic of a handfasting can be released and reversed by untying the knot that was fastened during the ceremony. It seems unlikely that in another lifetime, the cord that was tied at a past-life handfasting could be remembered and located in order to untie the knot and free you both from your commitment if necessary.

For some people, getting handfasted is stressful, and this apprehension can bring tension to a couple. Experiencing pre-handfasting anxiety does not mean that you need to reject the whole relationship or the idea of making a commitment. But pre-handfasting turmoil can make it difficult to separate your feelings for your future partner from feelings about the stress of planning.

Try to remember how you felt about your partner-to-be before the intensity of planning and preparation began. If the two of you have planned your magic well and reached agreements about the commitment you are making and your ceremony, it is unlikely that s/he is the problem. Keeping in mind a time when you had more clarity may help you distinguish your worries from your true feelings. You will very likely return to more positive feelings for your partner once the pressure of your ceremony is over.

3

The Date and Time

Some couples consider magical and/or astrological significances when selecting the date, time of day and location for their handfasting. Below are some common magical associations.

Lunar

Dark moon - introspection
Full moon - increased power
Waxing moon - increase
Waning moon - decrease

Solar/Day

Midnight - releasing
Sunrise - fresh beginnings
Noon - additional/building energy
Daytime - heightening/growing
Sunset - discharge
Night - reverse/diminish

Solar/Year

    Hallows - October 31 - depth/intensity
    Yule/Winter Solstice - December 21* - revitalization
    Bridget - February 2 - expansion
    Spring Equinox - March 21* - balance,
        moving toward growth
    May Day - May 1 - sexuality
    Summer Solstice - June 21* - sustained
        energy
    Lammas - August 21 - bounty
    Fall Equinox - September 21* - balance, moving toward decline
*The exact dates of the solstices and equinoxes vary from year to
year. Check an ephemeris, astrological calendar or almanac for dates
in a specific year.

Astrological Significance

    In addition to harmonizing various magical properties, you may
want to explore the astrological significance of specific dates. Many
people believe that planetary influences generate an actual energy. If
you agree, then the time, date and place of your handfasting can
suggest the future of your relationship. According to astrology, this
information can provide insights about the quality and outcomes of
your partnership. If you are familiar with astrology, you have probably considered the effects of particular dates. If you have no
knowledge of astrological influences, consider seeking the services of
a reputable astrologer. Tell the astrologer the possible dates and
locations of your handfasting, and ask for advice.

Practical Considerations about Scheduling

    Since early Grecian culture, May has been considered an
unlucky month to be married. Although most people do not know

why, even now this prohibition affects wedding plans. June is still the most popular month for conventional weddings, followed by the other summer months. However, many Pagans like to be handfasted in October so to begin the new Craft year as a fomally committed couple.

On a more mundane level, you will have to take into account the availability of potential handfasting sites. With the popularity of summer ceremonies, it is more difficult to find spaces and services during these months. June dates are generally the first to be booked, sometimes years in advance for popular venues.

Money-Saving Alternatives: Scheduling

◆ A handfasting is less expensive if you have it in one of the "off months" of November, December or January.

◆ The most expensive day to get married is Saturday. The most expensive time is Saturday at 7 p.m.

Of course, the first thing to check is what dates you and your partner have available. Look closely at your calendars and activities to see what they look like around the time(s) you are considering. Look at your work schedules. If you want to take vacation time before your handfasting to prepare either magically or on a practical level and you will also take vacation for a honeymoon, your work activities may help determine the timing of your ceremony. If you have children, checking their schedules can avoid conflicts with graduation, proms or Little League. You can alleviate potential scheduling problems by planning for you and your partner and key participants well in advance. And once you choose a date and time, make sure that all of these people put it on their calendars!

For many couples, a significant component of their handfasting is having family and friends share in the magic. If you want to be sure specific people are present, consider their schedules before you do too much planning. This is especially true for those you want to participate in the ritual or those who will act as attendants. You may not be able to plan your date around the schedule of every person you would like to attend, but you know the people you consider crucial.

Here are some things to keep in mind as you consider potential dates. Is anyone on your must-have list:

◆ Graduating?

◆ Pregnant? If so, when are they due?

◆ Planning a surgery, or are they ill? Will that affect their ability to attend?

◆ Traveling for work or pleasure around the date you are considering?

◆ In college? Does your date coincide with finals or other exams; the bar for law students or boards for medical students?

◆ Someone who has young children who are in school? Will it be hard for them to arrange a sitter for the children or to take them out of school to attend the ceremony?

You may also want to think about the weather around the date you are considering. Winter handfastings can be beautiful, but conditions may make it difficult or impossible for many of your guests to attend. If you are planning an outdoor ceremony, the height of summer may be too warm for comfort. Wedding planners tell horror stories of summer weddings where it is so hot the cake melts and slides into a pile, while guests faint from heat exhaustion. You know best what the seasons bring if your ritual is in your home area. If your handfasting is at some distance, check the weather there on the internet or with a local contact. Be sure to take the weather into consideration when selecting your date.

Some Dates to Avoid

In your planning process, you may want to avoid:

◆ Major Pagan holidays, such as Halloween. (People generally prefer to celebrate in their own circles on these occasions.)

◆ The two days when the time changes from standard to daylight savings and back again. People invariably make time mistakes on these days and will arrive early or late to your ritual.

◆ The date of any previous marriages or commitment ceremonies involving the partners-to-be.

◆ Any date close to a major family misfortune or death.

◆ For handfastings in the U.S., April 15.

◆ Also in the U.S., Memorial Day, Labor Day or Thanksgiving weekends. Travel complications on these holidays may keep your guests from arriving or even trying to attend.

◆ Any date that is near any other special time or event. For example, if you have children, it would be inconsiderate to have your handfasting on one of their birthdays.

4

The Place

As discussed in Chapter 3, some astrologers believe that choosing a place to be handfasted can affect the success of your union. There are several things to consider in site selection.

The first is to find a space that you like. Locations that you find beautiful and in which you feel comfortable can be your first priority. Talk with your future partner about what s/he envisions as the perfect place, keeping in mind that there is no need to rule out any environment. Handfastings can be held indoors or out, in rural homes or city parks, in traditional churches or at Pagan gatherings, even in your own backyard. Whatever you consider to be a magical environment that will help create a memorable handfasting is a possibility.

That having been said, there are things you should consider before selecting a location. Look at your guest list. Is the site con-

venient for those who will attend? You can be handfasted in
England on Glastonbury Tor, but if your attendants, family and
friends cannot come because of the distance, you may want to
reconsider. You may want to backpack to your handfasting on a
mountaintop, but if your 85-year old great-aunt simply must attend
or the occasion will be ruined, then reconsider. If there are people
with disabilities on your guest list, the accessibility of your site must
be a consideration.

Depending on the people you invite, accessibility issues may
include:

◆ Wheelchair access (including restrooms)

◆ Ability to maintain a visual line of sight for deaf or hard-of-
hearing people

◆ Attention to scents and other environmental elements
which may cause allergic reactions

◆ Appropriate lighting

◆ Some wider seating

◆ Space left among the seats for wheelchairs

If you would like someone to attend but are unsure of their
accessibility needs, ask them. Be tactful but straightforward. Explain
that you want them to come, participate and enjoy your ceremony,
and you need to know what arrangements they need. Anticipating
the needs of differently-abled guests and participants in advance and
accommodating them can forestall problems and ensure that these
guests are fully a part of your rite.

Tips and Trivia: Verification

◆ Confirm everything. Once you have made a reservation,
placed an order or hired a person, call them several times before
your handfasting. Politely verify with them what you are expecting
and confirm that they still intend to provide the service.

Handfasting Locations

One of the first steps in planning a wedding used to be re-
serving the church. However, more and more couples now select
non-traditional locations, even for conventional ceremonies. Some
couples want a place with a special association, such as the place
they met or some other significant spot. For others, the choice of
location may depend on scheduling conflicts at their preferred site.

Once you have made certain that the location you want is
available on the date and time you are planning, there are other
factors to consider.

Cost

Be certain that you clearly comprehend the cost that you will
be charged and what that cost includes for each space that you
consider. It is not uncommon for rental fees to be charged by the
hour. For example, a base rental for a location may make it yours for
three hours. There may an added fee for each extra hour or part of
an hour. Make certain you understand the fee schedule and any
additional charges you will be expected to pay.

Most couples need access to their space before the ceremony
to set up an altar and decorate. Check to be sure that the site will
be accessible to you, your florist or anyone else you designate
before the service. If the site has dressing rooms that you want to
use, make certain to specify your need for them during negotiations.

Ask how the various facilities handle clean-up. The rental of
some spaces includes custodial services, but find out if this is included in the basic cost or if there's an extra charge. Some facilities
expect you to clean the space before you leave. Understand what
the guidelines are and what rate you will be charged for set-up and
clean-up. Tell your contact person how much time will be used for
preparation and clean-up and how much time will be used for the

event itself. Many facilities have different fee schedules for set-up and cleaning activities.

Some "wedding chapels" include everything. If you are considering this kind of space, be sure to understand and get in writing which of their services you are required to use. Although many of these facilities are trustworthy, others charge for everything, including a minister, wedding coordinator or an organist, even if you don't use their services.

To avoid surprises, check if there are any other policies for your proposed space. For example, some elegant venues require designated clothing; some have restrictions about the type of flowers, music, candles or decorations they allow.

Certain places specify a time when all amplified sound must end. Additionally, some gardens and galleries regulate the type of photography and videography they allow. There may even be restrictions on what may be used for a farewell toss for the handfasting couple. Many places now prohibit the traditional tossing of rice, as rice can cause serious injury to birds who come by later and eat it. Some sites ask you not to toss glitter, birdseed or confetti. Find out what is allowed and provide a fun alternative for your guests.

If you want specific accessories for your ceremony, see if the space you have chosen already has these items on hand. Places that frequently host weddings often have canopies, aisle runners, candelabras and other ceremonial items. Or, you may find that not only do some venues not have these objects, they prohibit them or other elements that are important to you. If you want to mark the end of your ceremony by releasing a pair of lovebirds, make sure that your chosen site can accommodate them. Ask if you will be allowed to use any of the items that are important to you. Some spaces restrict candles due to melting wax, and some prohibit aisle runners or canopies because of how they must be anchored to the floor for safety reasons.

Some Additional Questions about Potential Sites

◆ Is the site beautiful, and does its energy feel good to you and your partner?

◆ Are there any other activities scheduled at this place on the same day? If so, at what time? Is there plenty of time and space for both the other activity and your handfasting?

◆ Is there enough room for all of your guests?

◆ Is the site handicapped accessible?

◆ Does it have air conditioning or adequate heating?

◆ How are the acoustics?

◆ Are there convenient and accessible restrooms that will be available to your guests?

◆ Will someone from the facility be there on the day of your handfasting? Will they have the authority (and the keys!) to resolve any problems that occur?

Home Handfastings

A private home can provide a lovely setting for a handfasting. This could be a parent's house, the home of a friend or even your own home. A home handfasting allows comfortable surroundings to be an integral part of the rite. The ceremony can take place in a large backyard or a romantic indoor area. Rental services can provide chairs for guests and other necessary items, and a caterer can reduce some of the burden on the homeowner.

Outdoor Handfastings

Many Pagans prefer to have rituals outside, and it is hard to surpass the beauty of nature. Places for an outdoor site include local parks, gardens or even your own backyard. If you want to be outdoors, consider renting a tent. Tents can be set up almost anywhere and provide protection from rain or sun. Using a tent ensures that no matter what the weather, your handfasting can take place in relative comfort. In most areas there are rental companies that deliver  and set up virtually any size tent. Tents come in a wide variety of colors, styles and sizes, with or without side panels. They vary in capacity from the most intimate to some that seat over 2000 and have dance floors.

There are many advantages to using an outdoor site. It often removes restrictions such as limits on the number of guests and limitations about decor, hours or menu that other sites impose. The limitations of an outdoor ceremony are probably obvious: insects, temperature, uninvited onlookers and many other possibilities can come into play. However, the beauty of outdoor sites can overcome many of these limitations.

Destination Handfastings

A destination handfasting takes place where you intend to honeymoon. These are also known as travel handfastings or honeymoon handfastings, and they offer many advantages. Foremost among these is the reduction in expense compared to a large ceremony and reception, because a far smaller group of guests — typically, only the attendants and a small number of close friends and family — attends. The handfasting couple pays the travel expenses of their Priest/ess, but the attendants and invited guests usually pay their own way. When possible, some handfasting couples or their parents offer to pay for some or all of the guests' expenses.

Other considerations for destination handfastings include local  laws and practices (for instance, if traveling in the U.S., can you bring a marriage license from your home state, or do you need to get one in the state in which you'll be hand-fasted? If the latter, what is involved in applying long distance for the license? Do you need a local contact to help with planning and arrangements? Can you make some of the arrangements through the internet?)

One potential problem at a destination handfasting can be elim-inated by taking any clothing or items for the ceremony in carry-on luggage when you travel by air.

Progressive Handfastings

Progressive handfastings occur over a period of time in different locations. If there are people in various locations with whom you want to celebrate or if you are planning a destination handfasting with only a few friends, you may want to hold additional recep-tions.

Progressive handfastings are the perfect solution for the couple with family and friends in various loca-tions. The actual ritual is held in the first phase, fol-lowed by a series of receptions in different areas. Those planning progressive handfastings need either to have lots of stamina or spread the events over a period of several weeks, as each occasion places additional responsibilities on the already active couple.

Preparing the Space

You may want to magically prepare the space you are using for your ceremony. This preparation magically cleanses the area and pre-sets the vibrations for the work to come. There are several ways to cleanse a site. The most common are asperging (sprinkling the area with salt water), censing (smudging with herbs/incense) or sweeping the area with magical intention. You may want to ask some or all of your attendants to perform this service, and be sure to discuss preparation with your Priest/ess to see if s/he prefers to do it him/her self.

Your Altar

Creating a beautiful altar for your handfasting is a significant part of your preparation. The altar at any ritual is a visual representation of the intent of the rite. Designing the look, purpose and essential elements of your handfasting altar, and then selecting or collecting items to carry out your vision, can be a fulfilling project.

You can create your altar with items from your personal collection that have special significance to you or you can purchase new objects that symbolize this new phase of your relationship. Whether you choose one of these options or a combination, your handfasting altar should be a visually pleasing and powerful centerpiece for your ceremony. If you need information about tools and other items that generally comprise an altar, talk with the Priest/ess who is performing your service.

It is essential to discuss with your Priest/ess her/his needs and preferences for the altar. S/he should be able to tell you what s/he will need, and you can combine this information with your own preferences to develop a list of what will be needed.

All of the ritual tools used do not necessarily need to be on a central altar. You can incorporate ritual objects into the decorations by placing them in the area of the circle where they will be used. For example, place the chalice on the West boundary of the circle and special rocks to the North. Be creative and produce an altar that is a visual delight for you and your guests.

Practical Decoration Issues

Consider the practical considerations involved in preparing your space. This includes seating, lighting and decorations that aren't necessarily required for the ritual but that beautify the area.

If your guests will be seated, check what type of seating is available when you reserve your site. If you want to create a circle, find out if you can move the seats and if the available space will allow all of your guests to be seated within. Verify with the space's contact person whether they provide chairs and tell them your seating design. In addition to a circle, other possible arrangements are seats in straight-across rows with an aisle or seats in a herringbone pattern of rows with aisles as needed.

If seating is not furnished by the facility or if you are planning your handfasting for a private home or outdoors, you may need to borrow chairs from your coven or rent them from a local rental service. Designate someone to make sure the chairs are set up in a timely manner and the way you envisioned.

Decorating the Space

Many couples personalize their handfasting space with special decorations which can include those seen at conventional weddings, such as flowers, candles, aisle runners, canopies and so forth. Some couples have an overall decorating scheme in mind, the theme of which is carried throughout their ceremony, including the color of gowns/tuxedos, altar items, even invitations.

Some popular themes are:

◆ A Victorian ceremony can include bustled gowns, high-button shoes, ribbons, bows, hearts and lots of lace.

◆ At a Black and White ceremony, everyone in the handfasting party is outfitted in black or white. Decorations and even flowers are black and white with occasional splashes of color.

◆ Period handfastings take their theme from a specific period in history. You could have a Greco-Roman, medieval, renaissance Elizabethan, Edwardian, Amazon or even an Old West handfasting.

◆ Holiday handfastings involve a ritual that coincides with a holiday. This might be a costume ball for a Hallows handfasting or a Yule ceremony complete with trees, holly, evergreens and candles or lights for decorations.

Some decorating and theme decisions are dictated by your budget and the location of your ceremony. Handfastings with complicated themes can be difficult to produce, but can also be impressive and memorable when done well. Clothing for theme weddings can be rented from local costume shops, borrowed from a theater company or sewn by you or a friend. Many bridal catalogs may have garments and decorations that fit well with your theme.

If you are being handfasted outdoors, many conventional decorating items can be beautifully blended into a natural setting. Tents and canopies take on an additional function, as they may be useful barriers to the sun or other elements. Floor runners may become the first line of defense against muddy clothes and shoes. Other considerations for outdoor handfastings are the comfort of your guests, screening your ceremony from the view of onlookers and how you can blend the beauty of the natural setting with your own decorating.

Tips and Trivia: Canopies

Wedding customs from many traditions include a canopy, which ensures that misguided spirits cannot interrupt the ceremony from above.

If your handfasting will be indoors, check with the facility or homeowner to see what type of decorations they allow. Many buildings have restrictions about tape, glitter and candle use. Before you begin serious planning, determine whether the decorations you prefer are allowed. Once you know what is possible, you can create a space for your handfasting using any of the objects discussed below or ideas of your own.

Conventional wedding planners say that incidents involving the aisle runner (a long piece of cloth that covers the walkway to the altar for the handfasting party) are the number one wedding-day disaster, and malfunctions can include the runners not unrolling properly or coming unfastened. Planners advise that if you use an aisle runner, make sure that the people who set it out understand how it works. You can even ask them to practice at the rehearsal and then roll the runner up again until the ceremony.

Flowers

Flowers are a hallmark of modern joining ceremonies, and are used in bouquets, corsages, boutonnieres and as decorations at the ritual and reception. With modern techniques, your floral options are endless. If you prefer not to arrange your own flowers or have a friend do this for you, a florist can help you decide what flowers will be best and create beautiful arrangements. Ask your friends or family about florists they have used or look for a florist whose work you like.

Tips and Trivia: Flowers
◆ Because orange blossoms are always green they are traditionally included in a bride's bouquet. Orange trees have both blossoms and fruit at the same time and are therefore a symbol of fertility and good fortune.

Money-Saving Alternatives: Flowers
◆ Use filler such as baby's breath or other greenery in the bouquet and decorations; the flowers themselves are the greatest expense.
◆ Ask several family members or special friends to each bring a personally selected, long-stemmed flower to the handfasting. Tie these flowers together with a ribbon and carry them as your bouquet.

Your florist will want to meet with you in advance to discuss your ideas and needs. Be prepared to make decisions about the color, mixture, number and type of arrangements you want, as well as the amount of money you are willing to spend.

Customarily, select a style of flowers that matches the overall style of your handfasting. If your ceremony is informal, casual flowers are best. If your handfasting is to be a formal occasion, formal flower arrangements can reflect this. (See Chapter 6 for more information about formal and informal handfastings.)

Your florist may also want to know if you would like fresh, dried or silk flowers. Although fresh flowers are beautiful, their beauty is short-lived. Some couples favor silk or dried flowers because they last indefinitely.

Money-Saving Alternatives: Flowers
◆ Instead of spending money on fresh flowers, rent silk flowers from a wedding supply store or local rental company.

Allow plenty of time for your first appointment with a florist. Bring swatches of dress fabric or pictures of the attendants' clothing if available. The style of clothing worn largely determines the form- ality of the rite (see The Clothes, Chapter 9) and can inform your florist, which can result in better advice to you. The kinds of flowers available may depend on the season. However, an accomplished florist can assist with selections that are available and within your budget.

Money-Saving Alternatives: Flowers
◆ Use greenery in large baskets to decorate large, open spaces or spaces you want to restrict. Look at a friend's farm or in the woods for greenery you can cut for free (with permission of course).

◆ Use flowers that are in season. Flowers flown in or grown in a hothouse are much more expensive.

◆ Ask a volunteer to take the flowers from your cere- mony to the reception to decorate the tables.

◆ Use flowers or greenery from your own garden or that of a friend or family member.

◆ Order flowers directly from a floral warehouse and ask a group of family or friends to arrange them the day before the handfasting.

◆ White flowers go farther than a similar number of colored blooms because white flowers stand out more and look larger than flowers of other colors.

Lighting

Consider whether or not your handfasting will require special lighting. For an indoor ceremony taking place before dark, this will probably not be a critical issue. However, for an outdoor rite as the sun is setting or after dark, lighting for safety as well as mood becomes a necessity. For an indoor evening ceremony, soft candlelight may be preferable to incandescent lighting.

There are many options both natural and artificial for lighting an outdoor ceremony, including torches, candles, luminaries, electric light strings or even firelight. Before making your lighting plans, check your ritual design for the number and location of activities that require light. If your Priest/ess or anyone else will read part of the ritual, create a lighting design that provides enough illumination for them to accomplish this in comfort. Consider visiting your site at the same time of day and in the same season as your ceremony is planned to give you a sense of what natural light will be available and what additional light you will need.

If you want candles for an outdoor ritual, have candles or holders that protect the flames from wind. Glass chimneys that enclose the candle, creating luminaries or using oil lamps that resemble candles can solve this problem.

Some things to keep in mind when designing lighting for outdoors:

◆ It is difficult for most people to read by firelight or candlelight.

◆ Flashlights may blind people and ruin the mood.

◆ Be sure to use only lights or extension cords approved for outdoor use.

◆ Check the area where people will gather and the path to and from your ritual site for lighting needs.

If you plan to have an open fire:

◆ Make sure your ritual will be held in an area where open fires are allowed. Check to see if you need a special permit.

◆ Make certain all ritual participants will fit in your circle when the fire is lit.

◆ Check the local weather for fire conditions.

◆ Ask a volunteer to bring a pail of water and a shovel to help in putting out the fire.

◆ Clear the fire area and create a barrier between the fire and other burnable materials.

◆ Ask someone to keep an eye on people in flammable clothing, and be sure that anyone with clothing that could accidentally brush against the fire (long sleeves, loose skirts) stays back from the flames.

5

Talking with
Non-Pagans

Talking with Non-Pagan Friends and Family

For some couples, parents or other family members can be the most challenging people to talk with about their handfasting. Unless Pagans raised you and your future partner, one or both of your families may object to your having this type of commitment ceremony.

It's best to tell your families about your religion before you tell them about your handfasting. If both subjects are introduced at the same time, family members may have trouble separating their feelings about Paganism from their feelings about a handfasting. Linking the two may result in a more volatile reaction than would otherwise have been the case.

Many people who don't know much about Paganism confuse it with Satanism.

Speaking to your family about your religion is an excellent opportunity to educate them and explain your faith and beliefs. This conversation may be all that is needed to suspend their apprehensions.

Most objections to handfastings fall into one of several categories, and if you consider these possible reactions, you can plan your responses.

It's a sin against God

If this is the issue and your family has a strong history of religious intolerance, it is probably best not to include them. When others hold these beliefs strongly, a continuing dialogue with them rarely brings understanding. However, if you have shared your religion before introducing the idea of handfasting, this can be an opportunity to remind your family about the beliefs of Paganism and explain why being handfasted is important to you. This kind of conversation can help non-Pagans feel more comfortable with and supportive of your decision.

It will kill your grandmother.

Although occasionally disputed, Paganism is not a word that kills. Grandma — or any older, close relative — is probably more resilient than your family thinks and may adjust just fine to your alternative ceremony. But if you think your family might be right, decide whether to include granny, and develop strategies for discussing your intentions with her.

What will our friends and neighbors think?

If your family is open to conversation on this, you can help them find ways to communicate with others about your handfasting and its importance to you. And remember, this is your handfasting, so don't succumb to family pressure to invite their friends and neighbors unless you truly want these people to attend.

It won't be "real"

For some people, a service that is not done by traditional clergy does not seem authentic. Remind your family that Paganism is a recognized religion in the United States, and as such its Priest/esses are granted the right to marry people under the law. If you get a marriage license, you can tell them that you have one and that your Priest/ess can legally sign it.

The Priest/ess who is performing the ceremony may be willing to meet with your family. Talking with her/him may eliminate some of their doubts, as s/he can answer their questions, communicate with them about their concerns and present another version of what clergy can be.

I have always dreamed of this day, and this is not what I had in mind

Find out what your parents' dreams involved. It may be possible to incorporate some or all of their vision in your ceremony. As long as their dreams don't conflict with your ideas or values, you may want to include them.

Remember, your ceremony should reflect your desires and dreams, not compromises to accommodate friends or family. If you find yourself bending to their will, reflect on the initial purpose of your ceremony and resolve to have it as you and your partner wish. This is the beginning of a new phase of your lives, and making these decisions (and sticking to them) can help signal this change.

The role that participants play in the ceremony is a consideration when deciding which friends or family to invite. All the people at a handfasting are asked to assist the Priest/ess in raising energy to seal the magic, so the guests should be considered, not only because of their relationship to the couple, but also in terms of their ability to lend magical support. A handfasting is first and foremost a magical rite. Remember to factor in the comfort level and familiarity with magic of those you invite.

There may be people you feel obligated to invite to your ceremony who you think either would not be comfortable assisting with a magical rite or would be uneasy attending a Pagan ceremony. There are several options to resolve this quandary:

◆ Have a different event that they can attend.

◆ Build explanations about what is going on and directions about how to participate into your service (see Appendix A for a sample of the use of a narrator).

◆ Invite only people you believe will enjoy and be comfortable at your handfasting.

◆ Have a separate secular ceremony.

Some couples have more than one ceremony. Even some of those having conventional ceremonies have one ceremony in one location and a second in another. Most people who do this treat the second service as a re-enactment. Instead of duplicating the wording and vows of the first ritual, the couple makes different statements such as, "I acknowledge that I have chosen this person as my partner." For those who want to adhere to strict, traditional protocol, at a second or subsequent ceremony none of the usual symbols of virginity such as a white dress or orange blossoms are worn.

Inviting non-Pagan friends and family to your handfasting can be a significant step in educating them about your religion. This exposure to Paganism may make an understanding and acceptance of the

Craft easier for all. Careful consideration of who can contribute positive energy to your union will help ensure its success.

Dealing with Non-Pagan Service Providers

It's up to you to decide how much to tell those who are providing handfasting services about the nature of your ceremony. In many instances (for example with a florist or a caterer), there may be no need to "come out" as Pagan unless you want to. In your interactions with them, there is probably little which will reveal you are not having a conventional wedding.

If a service provider will be present at the ceremony or any obvious part of your reception, find a way to let them know about your religious practices. They will provide the best service to you if they are not surprised by the nature of the ceremony in the middle of it, and, while you may have grounds to sue a photographer who walks out on a contract after discovering s/he is at a Pagan service, this will not be the same as having memorable pictures.

6

The Ceremony

What's the Difference Between a Conventional Wedding and a Handfasting?

The distinctions between a conventional wedding and a handfasting are myriad, starting with the roles of participants: the Priest/ess, the couple and the guests. In a conventional wedding, the rabbi, priest or minister is the one person responsible for creating and sealing the magic of the rite. You may be surprised to learn that standard marriages in religious settings are supposed to include magic. Those raised in Judeo-Christian religions were not taught to define acts of clergy as magic, but by strict definition, they are.

In keeping with patriarchal hierarchy, traditional Judeo-Christian marriage ceremonies call for the clergyperson to act as an intercessor between God and "man." S/he creates a link with God and draws on God's strength, authority and power to unite the couple. Each religion has a prescribed way in which this magic happens.

The role of a Priest/ess in a handfasting is quite different. S/he acts as a catalyst and focal point for the group, uniting divine energy with the energy of those present to assist the couple in creating their magical bond. S/he is an agent, selected by the handfasting couple, designated to facilitate the formalization of their magical connection.

First Decisions

Before you begin planning, you should have a very clear idea of the kind of handfasting you want. You will need to develop, at least in your head if not on paper, a detailed concept of how the whole day will unfold, which gives you a framework within which to make decisions and create the celebration you desire.

Search yourself to develop your concept of a perfect hand-fasting. Do you want to have a traditional ritual and reception with all the proper etiquette in place? Or a formal ceremony, complete with a lavish banquet? Perhaps you prefer an informal service in a garden, during which you and your attendants are barefoot.

People who have been married or handfasted before may want to consider how this second ritual can be different from the first. Think, visualize, talk and share with your partner and anyone else who is helping you plan. Don't forget it is your handfasting; the only other person whose opinion really counts is your partner-to-be. Explore your personal styles, tastes, imagination and ideas, and from these, create a ritual and celebration which reflect both of your dreams.

A handfasting couple has to make several decisions that other couples do not. You have to decide if you want your guests to sit or stand during your ritual. In conventional weddings, guests are usu-ally seated. However, in many Craft traditions, rituals are held with those-who-are-able standing throughout. Discuss with your Priest/ess her/his specific requirements or opinions. In most cases, it will be your choice. Take into account the length of your ceremony, the feasibility of having chairs at your site and the physical comfort of your guests.

Another decision is whether guests will be in a circle or rows for the service. In most conventional weddings, guests are seated in some semblance of rows, but most Pagan celebrations are held in circles. Again, consult with your Priest/ess for his/her suggestions.

This decision may be dictated by the size and shape of the space you choose. If the space configuration is not an issue, decide based on your personal preference. An experienced Priest/ess should be able to cast a circle no matter how participants are arranged.

One of the first considerations is how formal you want your ceremony to be. Many decisions, from the type of clothing worn to the kind of music played, are affected by this choice.

Traditionally, there are three wedding styles: formal, semi-formal and informal. The degree of formality is based on the style of dress worn, the kind of ceremony, the number of people who attend, the number of people in the wedding party and where the reception will be held. A general rule is that larger weddings with two hundred or more guests are most often considered formal. Weddings with more than seventy-five but fewer than two hundred fall in the semi-formal range, and those with fewer than seventy-five are in the informal sphere.

Formal weddings feature an elegant gown, tuxedos and refined flower arrangements. A semi-formal wedding has more flexibility in the type of clothing worn and in the decorations. Informal wedding cloth-

ing may include the most casual wear, such as blue jeans and sandals. Determining the level of formality guides you in selecting music, flowers, clothing and even a site to match your style. Make this decision before you plan too far, as it is one of the first questions asked by florists, caterers and clothing shops.

> ### Tips and Trivia: Trends
> Sophisticated simplicity in everything is the trend today. This simplicity involves the entire ambiance of events, encompassing clothes, cake, decorations and music, and affecting both the ceremony and the reception.

Components of a Handfasting

You can construct your handfasting in many ways. Following are some of the more common elements for you to consider, and you can add others that you like. The explanations below are brief; if you want more detailed information about any component, talk with your Priest/ess.

Music

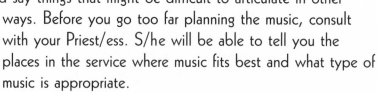

Music can be an important part of ritual and adds joy and texture to a reception. Your musical selections personalize your ceremony and say things that might be difficult to articulate in other ways. Before you go too far planning the music, consult with your Priest/ess. S/he will be able to tell you the places in the service where music fits best and what type of music is appropriate.

At formal services, there are usually six times when music is presented:

1. The Prelude: A prelude begins thirty minutes before the start of the ritual, supplying background music for guests to

be seated and helping create the mood.

2. The First Solo: Usually begun after the bride's mother is seated (at heterosexual handfastings), this song sets the tone of the service. In same-sex ceremonies, this solo can begin after both sets of parents are seated.

3. The Processional: A musical proclamation played while the handfasting couple and their attendants approach the altar.

4. The Second Solo: A song that is special to the handfasting couple, usually performed after the couple takes their vows.

5. The Recessional: Played as the couple leaves the altar, this piece should be an energetic celebration.

6. The Postlude: Background music for guests as they leave the ritual space.

Music at Informal Handfastings

At an informal handfasting, the amount of music, the selections and their placement are limited only by your imagination. Music can be inserted into the ritual at any point to add texture or interest to the service. At some informal handfastings, the couple even sing to one another.

Musicians

After you determine the type and amount of music you want, begin to look for musicians. Consider first your talented friends or family members, but if there is no one suitable you can hire musicians to perform.

Conventional weddings often have an organist or pianist who plays instrumental selections and accompanies a soloist. Choirs, madrigal groups and other vocal groups can take the place of the

standard soloist. Instrumental options are myriad. Harp, guitar, harp-
sichord, flute, or even brass or string ensembles add a distinctive
sound.

One of the best ways to find musicians is to ask people
you know or check a local wedding planning guide for
musicians who advertise. You can also call a nearby
music school or even a high school for referrals.

It is reasonable and acceptable to ask to hear musicians perform before you hire them, and many musicians will gladly
provide you with a tape or invite you to an upcoming performance
so you can check them out. To reduce the possibility for surprises on
the day of the handfasting, many couples also contract with their
musicians to attend the rehearsal and play the pieces they will perform at the points where those pieces fall in the service.

If you engage professional musicians, be certain you understand
everything that is included in their fees before signing the contract.
Musicians can be found at various costs, so spend some time search-
ing or negotiating to be sure the price is within your budget.

Musicians who play at the ceremony can be invited to attend
the reception, but they are generally paid in cash after the ceremony.
Similarly, musicians who perform at the reception are paid in cash
when the party's over. Ask a reliable volunteer to handle these tasks.

Money-Saving Alternatives: Music
◆ Instead of hiring professional musicians, ask talented
friends or family to provide the music for your ceremony.
◆ Call a local college or high school music department and
ask for recommendations of students to perform at your ceremony or reception.

Recorded or Taped Music

If you cannot hire live performers, you can use recorded or taped music. Make sure any equipment you intend to use has been checked and is in good operating order on the day of the event. Recheck the equipment once it has been moved to the location of the handfasting/reception. You should be able to find music for your handfasting in your own collection, the collections of friends, in local record stores or even in a public library.

Being Escorted Down the Aisle

Some couples look forward to having a family member walk one or both of them to the altar. This practice need not reflect the traditional "giving away of the bride" but can be a way to honor a family member or someone close to the couple. You can ask this person to represent all of the friends and family who will be asked to support your new union.

At a different-sex handfasting, tradition holds that the father of the bride walks his daughter down the aisle. "Traditions" for same-sex ceremonies have not yet been cast in stone, but one idea is for each person in the couple to be escorted down the aisle by a parent or someone close. Handfasters often ask other family members or a friend to walk with them. Unless you want to follow convention, this person need not be of a different sex from the person they are escorting.

If none of these appeals to you, don't worry. It is perfectly suitable for you and your partner to walk down the aisle alone or together. When you are considering whether or not to be escorted, imagine how nervous you think you will be and whether having someone with you as you walk toward the altar will be a blessing or not.

Pre-Ceremony Timeline

For those who want to have your guests greeted and seated in a conventional manner, the following timetable can provide useful guidelines.

◆ Forty-five minutes before the ceremony: Ushers assemble at the main entry to the ritual space and get their final instructions. If there are printed programs for the ceremony, they should be given to ushers at this time.

◆ Thirty minutes before the ceremony: The musical prelude begins. Ushers begin to escort guests to their seats.

◆ Twenty minutes before the ceremony: Participants in the ceremony who are not walking down the aisle (but who will wait at the altar while others walk down the aisle) and the Priest/ess assemble near the door they will enter. This is most conveniently done if there is a side room available off the altar area. This pre-ceremony staging is also when a chosen attendant should give the fee and the marriage license to the Priest/ess. If ushers will join the people in the side room, they should arrive there immediately before the processional begins

◆ Ten minutes before the ceremony: The grandparents of each handfaster and any parent not escorting a handfaster assemble at the main entry to the ritual space.

◆ Five minutes before the ceremony: Grandparents are escorted to their seats by ushers.

◆ Four minutes before the ceremony: Any parent not escorting a handfaster down the aisle is taken to their seat. For a different-sex handfasting, the mother of the bride is traditionally the last to be seated. For same-sex ceremonies, decisions about the order of seating these special guests can be made by the couple.

◆ Three minutes before the ceremony: The attendants in the handfasting party and parents or others who are escorting a handfaster assemble and prepare for the processional.

◆ Two minutes before the ceremony: If an aisle runner is being used, two ushers walk together to the front of the runner, unroll it and fasten it in place. If these ushers will stand with others at the altar, they should then proceed to the side room where the rest of the handfasting party is gathered. If these ushers will walk down the aisle, they return to the main entry where they will join the processional.

◆ Ceremony time: The participants in the side room enter the ritual space and stand in their places. When they are all in place, they turn to watch the processional. The processional begins.

Tips and Trivia: Programs

Some couples provide printed programs for their handfasting, listing the names of the attendants, the order of service and even poetry or other writings special to the couple.

The Conventional Order of a Processional

◆ Ushers who do not enter through the side door, usually walking down the aisle in pairs.

◆ Bridesmaids, who may walk individually or paired with another bridesmaid.

◆ The honor attendant, walking alone.

◆ The ring bearer and flower carrier.

◆ Each handfaster who is walking down the aisle and the person escorting them. (Traditionally, the handfaster takes the right arm of the escort.)

◆ Pages or trainbearers, if any (walking behind, carrying train/s).

Alternative Order of a Processional for Lesbian or Gay Couples

◆ Close friends or family of any gender who have acted as ushers.

◆ Close friends or family of any gender who have acted as attendants to the people in the couple.

◆ The rest of the processional as listed above, starting at the honor attendant.

Welcome and Introductions

Many couples welcome guests to their handfasting. This welcome can include introductions of people who need to be known (for example, a narrator) and information about what will occur during the ritual. The latter is especially important if non-Pagans or others unfamiliar with a handfasting attend.

Casting the Circle

A fundamental part of Pagan ceremony is casting a circle to contain the energy raised for the enactment of a ritual. A circle is usually cast by the Priest/ess, who walks around the area where the ritual will be held, enclosing the participants and any space or items that will be used.

Invocation

An invocation is the magical act of inviting the spirits of the elements (earth, air, fire, water and the God/dess) to a ritual. An invocation asks elemental energies and divinity to witness and attend. Invocations can be spoken, sung or enacted. Many Pagan couples honor friends and/or family by asking them to invoke an element. Some ideas for invocations are:

Lighting Incense

Many couples use the lighting of incense or herbs to invoke air/east and invite this element to their handfasting ritual. The incense or herbs can be placed either in the eastern area of the circle or on the east portion of an altar.

Sharing Bread/Cake

Couples often use bread or cake as a part of their invocation to earth/north. The loaf or cake is broken and each member of the handfasting couple feeds the other. As a way to honor guests, some handfasting couples share their bread/cake with those attending the ceremony.

Sharing Wine/Water

In some Pagan traditions, sharing water is the most sacred act. A chalice or goblet filled with water, wine or juice is held by one handfaster to the lips of the other while s/he sips the contents. This can be part of the invocation of water/west in ritual.

Unity Candle

The unity candle has become a common part of today's handfastings. It is created from three candles: one for each of the handfasters and a third, often larger, which serves as the unity candle. The first two candles are lit separately by the handfasters, and together they light the unity candle. Couples can do this as a part of invoking fire/south.

Attunement

Attunement can help bring participants fully into the moment and align them with the energy of the magic to be accomplished. Its primary purpose is to ground and center the participants, asking them to drop their daily concerns and focus on the magic.

Priest/esses carry out attunements in many ways, among them using a grounding exercise, guided visualization and verbal instructions.

Statement of Intention

It is important to verbalize clearly the goal of any ritual. A statement by the officiating Priest/ess about the purpose and intention of the rite can be just a sentence or two. For example, "We are gathered here today to witness the joining of (name) and (name). We ask this company assembled to share their energy and good wishes."

Exchanging Vows

The vows exchanged by you and your partner are your promises to one another, defining the commitment you are each making.

When planning vows, consider what you are willing to pledge. (See Chapter 2, The Purpose, for more discussion of the pledges that may be made in a handfasting.)

The conventional Christian wedding vow is, "I _____ take this woman/man to be my lawfully wedded husband/wife, to have and to hold from this day forward, for better or worse, for richer, for poorer, in sickness and in health, to honor and cherish, until death do us part." Even conventional Christian couples rarely use vows today that promise to "obey" their partner.

For a very personal touch, many couples write their vows, putting into their own words the promises they are making. (See Appendix G for more information on writing personal vows.) The exchange of vows is a time where you can express your individuality. Whether you decide on standard vows or those of your own creation, talk with your Priest/ess about this most important part of your ceremony.

Some couples keep their vows a secret from one another, not sharing them until the ritual. This is fine as long as what you say will not actually be a surprise. Long before the day of your handfasting, you both need to agree on the commitment you are making. You can discuss the content of your vows without disclosing the specific wording. A handfasting commitment is commonly phrased, "as long as we both shall love." For most couples, this by no means lessens the intent of their commitment.

Before you have put a lot of time and effort into creating your vows, check with your Priest/ess to see if s/he has any guidelines. Different traditions have different ideas about what is appropriate to say at the altar, and it is wise to discuss these issues well ahead of time.

More and more couples these days stand facing their family and friends during the ceremony, especially while they make their vows. Because the Priest/ess moves frequently during the course of the ceremony, it is usually not difficult for her/him to move to a position in front of the handfasting couple with his/her back to the guests. If this is something you want, tell your Priest/ess. You will not be able to face all of your guests all of the time if they are in a circle, where you will always be facing toward some people and away from others. But you can turn in different directions through the service to make contact with everyone.

Exchanging Rings

Exchanging rings has been a part of joining ceremonies for centuries, and many handfasting couples do this as well. Both members of the couple usually exchange rings, which can be done at any point, but is traditionally done right after vows are spoken. Rings can be set on the altar or held by one of the attendants until time for the exchange.

Tips and Trivia: Rings

◆ The continuous circle formed by a ring conveys unity and is said to act as a charm against misguided spirits.

◆ Many people consider it bad luck to remove your wedding ring — ever.

◆ Although expensive, platinum currently is the most popular choice for commitment rings. This is because it is quite durable as well as beautiful.

◆ A wedding ring is placed on the third finger of the left hand because ancient Egyptians believed a vein ran directly to the heart from this finger, giving this finger the power to remove adverse energy from anything it touched.

◆ Greek and Roman healers prepared prescriptions by stirring the mix with the third finger of their left hand, which would communicate to their heart if there was any problem with the ingredients.

◆ In some countries and ethnic heritages, commitment rings are worn on the fourth finger of the right hand. Couples in Germany wear engagement rings on their left hand and transfer them to their right hand during the ceremony.

◆ If you have been wearing an engagement ring, be sure to remove it before your ceremony if you intend to wear your commitment ring on the same finger.

Tying the Cord

One difference between a conventional wedding and a handfasting is suggested by the name. A handfasting couple's hands are literally fastened together. When energy has been raised, a cord is looped around the couple's joined hands and a knot is tied. This way of "binding" a marriage has been used for centuries and is the origin of the expression "tying the knot."

The practice of knot magic holds a respected place in Celtic customs and in many other cultures as well. A knot closes and holds magical intention.

To people unfamiliar with Craft traditions, tying a couple's
hands together may seem to imply dominance or
appear to be bondage, but this is not accurate.
Tying the knot is a magical act of joining two people, not an indication of subservience or imprison-
ment. Most couples slip off their handfasting cord
at the end of their ceremony. Some couples continue to wear the
cord during their reception.

Tips and Trivia: Knots and Cords

◆ For many centuries, the only way to join two things together was with a knot. Knots were a symbol of a bond that could not
be broken, and being able to tie a durable knot was considered a
magical act.

◆ At a conventional Mexican wedding, the bride is attended
by her four godmothers, each of whom is responsible for an element in the ceremony. One godmother makes three bouquets:
One is carried and kept by the bride, one is placed on the altar and
one is tossed to waiting friends at the reception. The second godmother is responsible for the rings which she carries on a dish
along with thirteen gold coins. The third and fourth godmothers
carry a rope that functions similarly to the cord used in a handfasting.

◆ Celtic custom was to loosen all knots on a wedding couple's clothing. In India, a similar convention makes certain that
every knot in a couple's attire is untied so that the only knot tied
on their wedding day is the one tied at their ceremony.

◆ A conventional bride's bouquet in Europe has ribbons, the
ends of which can be tied in knots. If someone who knows magic
prepares the bouquet, each knot can be a wish for the new bride.

◆ Most of us are familiar with the belief that the one who
catches a bride's bouquet will be the next to be married.
Another less-known belief is that untying one of the lover's knots
in the bouquet will make a wish come true.

Garland Crowns

In some Pagan traditions, the handfasting couple picks flowers on the day of their ceremony and makes garland crowns for each other. These blossoms are woven into floral circlets and exchanged during the handfasting.

Jumping the Broom

Jumping the broom is a standard feature at Pagan handfastings. A common-law marriage practice, jumping the broom was used for centuries as a way for couples to declare their union when no established religious authority was available. Jumping the broom in front of family and friends made their union official. African slaves in the U.S., whose owners usually did not allow them to marry legally, also jumped the broom, and the practice continues today in many African-American weddings.

Jumping the broom involves exactly what it says: A broom is held at a comfortable height or placed on the floor/ground, and the couple joins hands to leap over the broom together.

Recessional

A recessional is the formal exit of the handfasted couple after the Priest/ess has opened the circle. The attendants, the couple's parents and finally the guests follow the couple.

The Rehearsal

A rehearsal is usually held the evening before the ceremony and should be held when the Priest/ess who will officiate can be present. Allow enough time to practice, especially if you plan to have a dinner following the rehearsal. Rehearsals take anywhere from an hour to an hour-and-a-half, depending on the length and complexity of your service. The evening of the rehearsal is also a good time to give your marriage license to the Priest/ess, distribute checks to anyone who is being paid and give gifts to your attendants.

Usually the Priest/ess takes charge of the rehearsal. If this is not the case, you may want to appoint someone to organize the participants and move the rehearsal along. Plan to run through the entire ceremony.

Most Priest/esses do not say the ritual's actual words at the rehearsal, but the attendants, the handfasting couple, the Priest/ess and any other people involved all walk through their parts.

You can make sure that your rehearsal and consequently your ceremony go more smoothly if you take equivalents of any items that you'll use. This includes the items used to call the elements, a replica of the unity candle, the handfasting cord and perhaps even the rings. You can make "bouquets" out of ribbons from gifts that were opened at pre-handfasting showers to use at the rehearsal.

Many couples have a rehearsal dinner after the run-through. In conventional heterosexual marriages, the groom's family hosts and pays for the rehearsal dinner, and there is a standard guest list. Same-sex couples can also follow the invitation guidelines. Invite everyone who attended the rehearsal and their partner/s, including the Priest/ess and his/her partner. The parents of any children who participate in the ceremony are customarily invited as well. If the children are too young to appreciate a prolonged dinner, the handfasting couple may arrange for a sitter to stay with them. Relatives of either handfaster who have come from out of town (including parents and grandparents) are usually invited. Last but not least, invite any friends who you think are appropriate to include or who you would simply like to have present at your dinner.

Tips and Trivia: Insurance

Wedding insurance can be purchased to cover canceled weddings, photography catastrophes and personal liabilities.

Tips and Trivia: Name Changes

In most states, in handfastings involving persons of the opposite sex, either person may change any or all or none of their legal name.

Any one can legally change their name. An attorney can assist you with changing your name to any name that you choose.

Tips and Trivia: Places to Inform of Your New Name:

◆ The state agency that issues your driver's license and vehicle registration

◆ The bank, including checking, savings and investment accounts

◆ The Social Security Administration

◆ The Internal Revenue Service

◆ The agent of any trusts, wills or guardianships in which you are named

◆ The register of deeds for your house

◆ Insurance agencies

◆ Your employer

◆ Your doctor and dentist

◆ Passport officials

◆ The library

◆ The phone, cable and utility companies

◆ Your state voter-registration agency

◆ Magazine subscriptions

◆ Motorist assistance programs (like AAA)

◆ Professional and social organizations
◆ Your computer accounts
◆ And don't forget to tell your family and friends!

7

The Priest/ess

One of the most important decisions to make is choosing the person who will perform the ceremony. This person flavors the entire occasion.

What do you see when you visualize your handfasting? Is the Priest/ess a female, a male or one of each? Does s/he have a formal manner or is s/he more casual? Does s/he have a conventional or alternative look? After you have answered these questions, check on what your future partner envisions. If you find differences, discuss what each of you wants and reach an understanding. Once you both agree on the qualities you want, you can begin identifying and interviewing candidates.

If you do not have a Priest/ess with whom you have regular contact, there are several ways to find one. You can:

◆ ask your friends
◆ look in Goddess, Pagan or new-age publications
◆ advertise in the Goddess, Pagan or new-age press
◆ call Pagan groups with which you are acquainted
◆ check Pagan resource directories
◆ do an internet search
◆ check with The Re-formed Congregation of the Goddess, International Office, Covenant of the Goddess or your local Unitarian Fellowship

After you have identified one or more prospective Priest/esses, set up a time to meet. You and your partner can explain what you want in your ceremony, discuss the date you have in mind, what tradition the Priest/ess follows and how much s/he charges. Let each Priest/ess know how much you want to be involved in the planning, whether you want input on the order and content of the ceremony, if you intend to write your vows and any other information you feel may be important. Listen carefully to the responses. This is your ritual, and within reasonable bounds, you should not have to compromise.

You may want to look for another Priest/ess if the one you're interviewing expresses any of the following:
◆ There is only one way the ceremony can be done.
◆ You have to do it her/his way.
◆ It is always done a certain way.
◆ You can have no or minimal input into the ceremony.
◆ S/he does not pay attention to your ideas/needs.

The personal chemistry between the two of you and the Priest/ess is one of the most important factors. Both of you should feel comfortable with the person(s) you choose. Ask questions about the knowledge, tradition and experience of each Priest/ess. Try to get a sense of his/her individual magical work. Having this information may make your decision for you.

Don't be surprised if your Priest/ess asks you to take part in ministerial counseling before your handfasting. In many traditions, counseling is one of the responsibilities of the Priest/ess, who must ensure that the people involved understand the commitment they are making and do not take their pledge casually. Magically bonding two people has profound ramifications, and most Priest/esses take this responsibility very seriously.

In counseling, the Priest/ess will explain the significance of being handfasted and will determine that each participant truly wants to be handfasted and no one is under duress. Whether or not the counseling extends beyond these basic issues depends on the needs of the Priest/ess and the handfasters.

Some couples are fortunate enough to have more than one person they would like to perform their handfasting. If this includes you, make certain that all officiants meet or otherwise communicate before the service, agree which part each will perform, compare their liturgies, consider your wishes and come to agreements that satisfy everyone.

Although you may have the training and experience to officiate at your own handfasting, it is difficult and complicated to switch roles at such a powerful time. Each member of the couple has specific responsibilities and magical duties, and on this special day, you might want to focus exclusively on your beloved and the commitment you are making. If you intend to register your union, in most states it is illegal for the officiant to be a one of the people in the handfasting couple.

Priest/ess are usually paid for performing a handfasting. The amount can range from $20 to $2000, depending on the area and the Priest/ess' training and experience. At your initial interview, ask what the Priest/ess charges. Many Priest/esses prefer that you make a donation to the religious organization with which they are associated, rather than pay them. If this is the case, you might want to also give your Priest/ess a personal, non-financial gift. In some areas, it is common to buy your Priest/ess a gift as well as pay them. If you are from a small coven and your Priest/ess is a close friend, it may be appropriate to give her/him only a gift.

Dealing with the charges and expectations during the planning stage can eliminate embarrassing moments later.

Some Questions to Ask a Priest/ess

◆ Have you done handfastings before? How many? How often?

◆ Is your schedule open on the date and time of the handfasting?

◆ Do you plan to do anything else that day (for example, another service) which might crowd your time?

◆ Are you willing to perform rituals outdoors, at someone's home or in another city or state?

◆ What parts of the ritual may we design?

◆ May we write our own vows?

◆ Are you licensed to perform legal marriages in the state where the handfasting will take place?

◆ May our children be part of the ceremony?

◆ What is your fee? Do you require this fee to be in the form of a donation? If so, to what organization?

◆ What documentation do you need to see? (A marriage license?)

◆ Will you want us to take part in counseling before the ceremony?

◆ How many times will you expect us to meet with you?

◆ Will you consider performing an interfaith ceremony where one of the officiants is not Pagan? Do you have any restrictions on conducting a ritual with another religious leader?

Questions to Ask Yourself about a Candidate for Priest/ess

◆ Does this person seem to have a connection to divinity?

◆ Does he/she seem capable of performing magic?

◆ Do you like her/him?

◆ Do you feel comfortable with her/him?

◆ Is s/he someone who can present her/himself well?

◆ Does s/he speak well? Do you like her/his voice?

◆ Did s/he ask you questions that you felt were appropriate about your spiritual beliefs?

◆ Did you feel any pressure or insistence to be a member of the Priest/ess' tradition?

Can a Priest/ess Conduct a "Conventional" Wedding?

Of course. If you and your future partner want a conventional ceremony, talk with your Priest/ess. Explain the type of ritual you would like. If s/he does not agree or seems uncomfortable with the idea, you may want to rethink your ideas or look for another clergy-person for your service.

8

The Attendants and Witnesses

Who and how many people will "stand up" with you at your handfasting are matters of personal preference. You can have several attendants or none. You may want to consider the comfort level and familiarity with magical ritual of any people you consider as attendants.

There are two major reasons to have attendants: to honor your friends or family by asking them to participate in a sacred ceremony and to ask those you trust for help. Many attendants take a lead role in helping organize a handfasting and the reception. Their duties can range from consultant to set-up crew. They can help dress the handfasting couple, monitor time constraints and provide moral support.

Tips and Trivia: Witnesses
◆ In ancient Rome, a minimum of ten people had to witness a wedding for it to be legal.

Attendants can take a prominent part in establishing ritual dynamics. They can be asked to call the elements, assist the Priest/ess or prepare the space. Attendants can accompany the handfasting couple or help seat guests. You can ask your Priest/ess to perform all the magical duties in your service or you can distribute these responsibilities among your attendants, family or friends.

Before proceeding, it may be helpful to discuss gender issues. In the past, the titles and duties of attendants were very sex-role-specific. The "groom" chose male attendants while the "bride" chose female attendants. For many couples, especially same-sex couples, the sex of attendants is not a concern. Having an attendant of another sex is quite common today. Even couples in a conventional ceremony choose people of another sex as attendants. Although this may be confusing to those who do not view gender as fluid, a man whose best friend is a woman can ask her to serve as his "best man" or a woman may ask a male best friend to serve as "maid of honor." When these titles don't work you can use others, such as primary attendant, honor attendant or primary witness. Don't worry about the opinions of others; speak with your partner to make certain s/he agrees, and bestow these honors on those you want.

Usually both handfasters have an equal number of attendants, and they are paired for certain activities during the ritual. For example, the two primary attendants follow the handfasted couple down the aisle after the ceremony. The rest of the attendants follow them. If you are making unconventional gender assignments for your attendants and you will pair them for certain activities, be sure they are aware of this decision and are comfortable with your requests.

Each person in the couple chooses his/her own attendants. Attendants at a conventional ceremony might include a maid or matron of honor, best man, groomsmen, ushers, bridesmaids, ring bearer and flower carrier(s). Additional positions to consider for a handfasting are summoner/herald, narrator, bard, guardian, bell ringers and those who call the directions. The duties assigned to attendants are up to you. There are, however, traditions about the responsibilities of attendants, especially the primary or honor attendants.

Tips and Trivia: Attendants

◆ In some countries, misguided spirits are believed to lurk on the periphery of weddings, hoping to attach themselves to the new couple. As many as ten witnesses who are dressed similarly to the wedding party should be in attendance to confuse these spirits.

Primary Attendants (Maid/Matron of Honor and Best Man)

In a conventional heterosexual couple, the bride's primary attendant is called a maid or matron of honor and the groom's is called the best man. (The duties are the same for either a maid or matron of honor. The marital status of the person you select determines the title: A single person is called a maid of honor, while a married person is called a matron of honor.)

Many people ask a sibling to be their primary attendant. But if you feel your sibling would be uncomfortable in such a prominent role at a Pagan ceremony or you are uneasy singling one sibling out among several, consider choosing a friend. Some people ask a parent to serve as their primary attendant. There are no rules about who should be the primary attendant, so ask anyone you want who is willing stand up with you during your ceremony.

By convention, the duties shared between the primary attendants are:

◆ Help choose the clothing for the handfasting.

◆ Help organize fitting schedules for other attendants.

◆ Help other attendants get shoes and accessories.

◆ Assist in arranging to pay for other attendants' handfasting clothing.

◆ Provide support; act as an advisor, messenger or secretary.

◆ Plan a shower or bachelor party.

◆ Organize the pick-up of any rented clothing and/or accessories.

◆ Keep the rehearsal on schedule and supervise the other attendants.

◆ Stay with each person in the couple on the day of the ceremony.

◆ Provide calm, support and assurance before the ceremony.

◆ Arrive early on the day of the handfasting to help the handfasters get dressed.

◆ Make sure handfasters' accessories are present and worn correctly.

◆ Drive or make arrangements for the handfasters' transportation to the ceremony.

◆ Bring ring/s to the ceremony.

◆ Distribute flowers to attendants and the handfasting couple.

◆ Run errands or make necessary phone calls.

◆ Participate in group photos.

◆ Lift veil/s of handfaster/s during the ceremony.

◆ Hold bouquet/s and rings during the ceremony.

◆ Straighten the trains on gowns.

◆ Participate in the ceremony in whatever way the handfasting couple has asked.

◆ Witness the handfasting couple's signing of the marriage certificate.

◆ Participate in the receiving line.

◆ Greet and make guests comfortable at the reception.

◆ Propose the first toast at the reception extolling the couple and their love for one another.

◆ Drive or arrange for the couple's transportation after the reception.

◆ Return or arrange for the return of any rented clothing and accessories.

◆ Pay for their own travel, lodging, clothing and accessories.

Other attendants' duties are similar to those of the honor attendants, and they are expected to assist in most of the same tasks, but to a lesser degree. Some differences are:

◆ The honor attendant plans a shower or bachelor party, and an attendant assists and attends.

◆ A primary attendant makes arrangements for ordering clothing and accessories, while other attendants provide assistance and personal information about dress or shoe size and any other pertinent data.

If you are not an honor attendant, chances are you can help most by asking the handfaster and the honor attendants what type of assistance they require.

Tips and Trivia: Position of Bride and Groom
◆ It is a custom for a bride to stand to the left of the groom in a heterosexual ceremony. This is believed to have come from the time when some marriages involved the capture and forced

presence of the bride, and a groom needed his right hand to be free so that he could draw his sword if necessary. During this time, a best man was considered the groom's "second" who stood somewhat behind the groom and to his right. This tradition is still practiced today.

Ushers

You may have the same attendants who stand with you during the ceremony act as your ushers, or you may want separate groups of people for each position. The duties are distinct: Attendants stand beside a handfaster during the ceremony and ushers assist with seating guests. If you want different people to do these tasks, make sure you are clear with them about the nature of your request and your expectations.

Other Participants:
Summoner/Herald

Depending on the location of your handfasting, you may want to designate a summoner, particularly if your handfasting will take

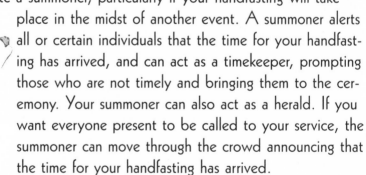

place in the midst of another event. A summoner alerts all or certain individuals that the time for your handfasting has arrived, and can act as a timekeeper, prompting those who are not timely and bringing them to the ceremony. Your summoner can also act as a herald. If you want everyone present to be called to your service, the summoner can move through the crowd announcing that the time for your handfasting has arrived.

Narrator

A narrator can be helpful, especially for the people who are not familiar with Pagan ceremony. At points in your service where there might be confusion, a narrator can explain what will happen and what is expected of participants.

Bard

If you want music at your ritual, you can designate a bard. If music is not an interest of yours but you want music at your handfasting, you can authorize your bard to be the musical director. Discuss with your bard the points where you want music and then turn the musical decisions over to her/him. If you want to select the music yourself, a bard can find the performers and instruments to accomplish your choices.

Guardian

Particularly if you will have your ceremony in a public place, you may want to ask someone or a group of people to be guardians. Guardians have many functions, but the primary one is to ensure the security of the space where the ritual takes place. If you use a public place, you could draw a crowd who may or may not be friendly, and even if friendly, onlookers may be disruptive. Posting guardians can help minimize problems.

Check with your Priest/ess to see if s/he wants the assistance of a Guardian of the Rite or several guardians to support the energy of the circle.

Ringers

Bell ringers are usually children who move through the ritual space, ringing delicate glass bells to announce the beginning of the service.

A Handfasting with No Attendants

You may decide not to have any attendants. If you do not want to be accompanied at the altar, be certain to arrange for someone to handle duties that attendants would have performed. If you have a marriage license, be certain to arrange for witnesses to sign it.

Attendants' Gifts

Couples customarily give gifts to the people who serve as their attendants, and often the same gift is given to all. You may select anything within your budget as your gift. It is, however, customary to give something that is commemorative and personal.

9

The Clothes

For some people, deciding what to wear at their handfasting is part of the fun, and for others, it is a detail that makes the experience difficult or tedious. Any and every type of clothing is appropriate. Some couples dress in conventional wedding clothes, while others are skyclad (naked) and others have chosen all variations in between. If you have always dreamed of walking down the aisle toward someone in a tuxedo and your experience will not seem complete without this, then discuss your dream with your partner-to-be to see if you can agree.

Selecting clothing is one of the first things a couple needs to consider. What will you both wear? What will your attendants wear? Do you want everyone's outfits to match, or do you want each person to be able to express her/his own tastes? It may come as a surprise that it is the wedding

gown that determines the style of a wedding by setting the tone for the rest of the wedding party and indicating the formality of the service, according to professional wedding planners. Everything from the bouquet to the type of decorations follows the lead set by the gown. Shopping for a gown, therefore, takes on an importance that you may not have anticipated.

If either or both of you wear a traditional bridal gown, it takes time to select and have one fitted or made. Professionals advise selecting your gown at least six months before the ceremony's date, which means you need to begin shopping even earlier. You can get ideas for gowns from magazines, wedding planning guides (available free in most large cities) and by checking at wedding shops.

Purchase prices of wedding dresses vary widely, and you can expect to spend at least $300 for a formal gown. If you know how to sew or know someone who can, the amount you spend depends largely on the materials you choose. Making your gown allows you to create a dress that is exactly what you want and is a perfect fit.

Tips and Trivia: Styles of Dress

◆ Formal: Floor-length gowns or cocktail-length dresses; black or white tuxedos with ties; or morning coats. The reception includes a sit-down dinner or a tasteful buffet.

◆ Semi-formal: Floor-length or cocktail-length dresses; dark formal suits or dark dinner jackets. The reception includes a sit-down dinner or light buffet.

◆ Informal: The attendants wear dresses of the same make, color and length as those of the handfaster; suits worn match the season. The reception includes a casual buffet.

If you want attendants to wear tuxedos, glance through magazines or go to a formal-wear shop for ideas of the type, style and levels of formality available. Tuxedos come in many colors, and some have fabrics designed to provide subtle accents. Color can be introduced into the traditional black tuxedo by a cummerbund, vest or tie.

Similar to shopping for a gown, select the tuxedos several months before your handfasting. To coordinate colors, take along samples of fabrics that will be worn by attendants. If some of the people who will wear tuxedos are out-of-town, the formal-wear shop can usually provide forms to record their key measurements.

Rented tuxedos can typically be picked up the day before the ceremony and are returned the next business day. You may want to ask one of your attendants to do this task, especially if you leave the reception for your honeymoon.

While planning what to wear, remember to consider the shoes and accessories. A veil is a conventional addition to a bridal gown. You may also want to find shoes, stockings/socks or gloves that complement the rest of your clothing. Remember, shoes should be comfortable. You will spend a lot of time on your feet the day of your handfasting, especially if you stand during the ceremony.

Consider the jewelry that you will wear. A general rule is, if the rest of your clothing is fancy, keep your jewelry simple; if your clothing is plain, you can accessorize with ornate jewelry.

Tips and Trivia: Diamonds

◆ There is an ancient belief that a diamond carried within it a sparkle that was a "flame of love." From this tradition, diamonds became the stone of choice for engagement rings.

When planning your clothing, think about how you want your

hair, nails and/or makeup to look. Each of these is a matter of personal choice. You may prefer a totally natural look or one that takes days to put together. Thinking about the way you want to appear at your handfasting well in advance will prevent hurrying around in the days before the ceremony, trying to make decisions and appointments.

Internet Shopping

The internet can play a large part in your shopping. If you are a very small or very large person, if you are planning a specific type of handfasting or if you are in an isolated area, you may find what you want online. Almost anything you need, from designer gowns to same-sex cake toppers, is available on the web. While you are surfing around the internet, remember to check for online gift registries, decorations and attendant gifts.

Some words of caution: When you buy items online, order them well in advance. Some things that seem on your monitor to be exactly what you want can turn out to be nothing like what you expected. Ordering early gives you a chance to see, touch and try on the item to be sure it is what you anticipated.

Tips and Trivia: Bridal Clothing

◆ In some rural European communities, it is traditional at heterosexual weddings for a bride to carry a handkerchief to catch any tears. These communities consider it lucky for a bride to cry on her wedding day. Her tears are thought to bring rain and ensure that she will never cry another tear over her relationship.

◆ According to the old rhyme, a wise bride traditionally has something old, something new, something borrowed, something blue and a lucky penny in her shoe when she walks down the aisle. This combination

ensures luck, prosperity and happiness for the marriage. The borrowed item is usually something from a happily married friend or
relative.

Attendants' Clothes

Back in the day, people believed that misguided spirits attended weddings and attached themselves to newly married couples.
The attendants' function was to confuse these spirits about who was
actually being handfasted. The similarity of clothing worn by attendants further confused these spirits so the couple could more easily
escape.

Whether you believe in misguided spirits or not, you may want
to have your attendants dress in clothing similar to yours and your
partner's. This, of course, is not required. You may dress attendants
in whatever clothing you desire and which they agree to wear. This
can mean anything from all attendants in entirely matching attire to
all attendants wearing shades of blue to everyone wearing different
colors and styles.

When you can, shop with your attendants for their clothing.
This gives you a chance to see how they look in the outfits you are
considering and hear their opinions about designs. If the attendants
cannot accompany you, keep in mind how they may look in the
clothing that you select. Since most attendants pay for their own
clothing, considering the cost and the possibility of subsequent wear
is courteous.

Clothing and accessories are ways to express your individual
style. Don't be afraid to wear what you want. It's more important
for you to be comfortable than it is to accede to societal standards.
Be creative, be yourself and attend your handfasting in clothing of
which you are delighted and proud.

Tips and Trivia: More about Bridal Clothing

◆ The belief that it's bad luck for a couple to see each other on their wedding day before the ceremony stems from the custom of arranged marriages, where the members of the couple usually did not know or see each other beforehand. In some areas, it is considered unlucky for the groom to see the bride in her wedding dress before the ceremony.

◆ Brides in Western cultures wear white to symbolize their purity. In many parts of Asia, the bride's wedding dress is customarily black.

◆ Many consider wearing a veil to be a magical act, believing that the person under the veil transforms from the person they were into the person they will become.

10

Second Weddings

Statistics indicate that about fifty percent of today's marriages are second marriages for at least one person in the couple.
Preparing to make another commitment may
conjure old feelings or memories. You may
remember your first partner and the vows
you shared, which can raise doubts about
the validity of vows and even cause you to
question your ability to make and keep a
promise. These questions are not uncommon
for those who make more than one commitment over the course of their lives. Even
people who love their partner and are truly
dedicated to their relationship can question
why making a public declaration is important
and if this is something they can follow
through with. It's better to face your fears
and deal with your concerns well before the
ceremony. Confronting your anxieties as they
surface allows you to move toward your
handfasting with grace and knowledge.

Probably the most common concern among the previously committed is that they expected the earlier relationship to last forever.
Exploring who you are now and what you have learned can be useful in establishing the differences that are true for this time.
Remember, you are a different person from whom you were before.
Pausing to evaluate what you have learned from your previous rela-
tionship/s may help establish a firm foundation for your current
pledge.

First, whether it has been months or years since your previous
commitments, you are older now. If you made vows when you were
very young, remember how you have changed, grown and what you
have learned about yourself. You may have lost some of your
naiveté and now have a stronger personal identity. Many people
find that as they approach another commitment, they have increased

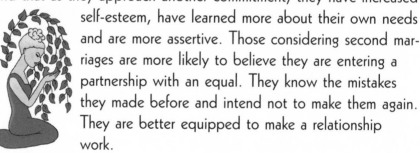

self-esteem, have learned more about their own needs
and are more assertive. Those considering second marriages are more likely to believe they are entering a
partnership with an equal. They know the mistakes
they made before and intend not to make them again.
They are better equipped to make a relationship
work.

The "you" you are today is planning this handfasting and a new
life with a new partner. This commitment to this partner is unique,
and you can count on it being different from previous commitments.

Don't try to create a ceremony that is "better than" your first.
This makes your first commitment become part of your second and
brings a perspective that is not healthy and not fair to you and your
new partner. View your coming commitment as a brand-new event
so that you can approach it with vitality and honesty. Anything less
does not bring the right magic to your handfasting or your union.

Many people are genuinely grateful that their previous relationship is over. Although most people say that they tried to make it work, they also know that they were not sincerely happy. These same people are first to agree that ending their preceding relationship/s was difficult, but once they accepted its end, they emerged with a truer sense of who they are and what they want.

Before looking more into concerns about an approaching handfasting, you may want to explore problem areas in your previous relationship/s and your reactions to them. Did you escalate situations or bury your feelings? When you were not pleased with your partner, could you have behaved differently? Do you recognize your responsibility for the end of your relationship? What behaviors and actions would you change and what would you keep?

Psychologists list the most common problems in failed commitments as:
◆ Not listening
◆ Not talking
◆ Expecting your partner to change and/or trying to change them
◆ Not communicating your thoughts and feelings, particularly about your relationship
◆ Being dependent on your partner or allowing your partner to become the focus of your life
◆ Inability to fight productively
◆ Controlling your partner or allowing yourself to be controlled
◆ Abusing your partner or allowing yourself to be abused
◆ Not considering your partner's needs and/or allowing your partner to be inconsiderate of your needs
◆ Suppressing your own needs to get along with or please your partner

◆ Behaving selfishly

◆ Letting routine drive excitement out of your relationship

◆ Keeping secrets from your partner, especially about the
past

◆ Low self-esteem on the part of one or both partners, which
leads to beliefs of inequality

◆ Lying to, betraying or manipulating a partner

Anxiety about your ability to make and keep a commitment tells
you that you love and value your partner and you want your relationship with him/her to last. It says that you are looking for ways to
strengthen the bond you share so it will endure for a lifetime.
Realizing this and knowing you are not doomed to repeat previous
failures can give you the strength and determination you need to
make this relationship a success.

Many people marrying a second time feel that their first ceremony was not really their own. Often, parents had the final say
about decisions based on finances, family and personal
concerns, and so what emerged may have borne little
resemblance to the couple's desires. Plus, first ceremonies often involve young couples who are more willing to let others influence their decisions.

Try to think of your first ceremony as an asset in creating your
second. This can be especially helpful if your first wedding was not
a handfasting. It's really not going to be the same this time. You
have experience with the process, you know what mistakes you
made before and what aspects of the ceremony need particular
attention. You are more likely now to know what you want and
don't want. Thank your previous experience for these insights.

Death of a Partner

If your previous commitment ended because of your partner's death, you may have conflicting emotions as you approach a subsequent commitment. Although you may feel true love for your new partner, you may feel that you are betraying your departed mate in some way. You may have made promises for a lifetime, and beginning a new life with someone else may feel like a betrayal.

It is important to go on with your life no matter what happened to your previous partner. Life is a gift from the Goddess, and it is incumbent on us to create as much love in our lives as we can. Although making another commitment may be intimidating, it is important for those of us who go on living to go on loving.

Traditions for Second Marriages

Because the large number of second weddings is a recent trend, conventions and traditions have not been firmly established. Large or small, formal or informal handfastings are all appropriate. One member of the couple may walk down the aisle with someone or handfasters may walk in together. Some couples, particularly those where one member of the couple has been recently divorced or widowed, announce only their handfasting and do not announce their engagement.

Tips and Trivia: Degrees of Formality

◆ Interestingly, the degree of formality at weddings and handfastings tends to diminish as the age of the handfasters increases. Fifty-one percent of people between ages 18 and 25 have formal ceremonies while only 14 percent of those 36 and over choose formality.

Children

Changing definitions of family have made it increasingly common for one or both handfasters to have children. Wedding experts say

that 64% of those marrying a second time have children. If you have children, you're not planning a handfasting for just the two of you, you're planning a ceremony that will join two families.

Couples with children often involve their children in the ceremony. Children can make an easier transition when they feel they are a special part of things. Children can walk one or more of their parents down the aisle, provide some of the music or readings during the ceremony, act as an attendant or take part in any other activity you feel is appropriate and they're comfortable performing. Any attendant's position is appropriate for a child, or you may want to acknowledge your commitment to your children as a part of your ritual. (See Appendix A: A Handfasting Ceremony for Couples Wishing to Acknowledge their Children)

Potential Roles for Children in Their Parents' Handfastings

They may:
- ◆ act as a ring bearer or flower carrier
- ◆ read poetry
- ◆ sing a song or perform an instrumental selection
- ◆ call the directions
- ◆ walk one or both of you down the aisle
- ◆ assist with lighting the unity candle
- ◆ stand with you at the altar
- ◆ participate in family vows

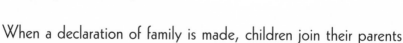

When a declaration of family is made, children join their parents at the altar and are introduced to the assembled guests. Some couples make pledges to their children as a way of recognizing their status as a family member.

No matter what the ages of your children, one of the few things on which all advisers agree is children should be the first to know about an engagement or plans for a ceremony. Even your adult children may have difficulty accepting your intention to take a new partner. Informing them of your decision well in advance, making sure they are among the very first to know and sharing your excitement with them can help ease the transition.

Recommitments

Some couples who have been together for a year or more have a ceremony to signal their recommitment to their relationship. There are many reasons why. Some Pagan couples make their commitment for a year and a day. When this time is over, they evaluate their relationship and decide if they wish to continue. A decision to continue can be recognized by a recommitment ceremony.

If you and your partner did not include magic in your handfasting or wedding, you can recommit to each other in a magical context. For some couples, a recommitment is a ceremony that honors their relationship; for others, it is a way to state a change in the nature of their commitment to each other.

If you are contemplating a recommitment ritual, considering the following questions may be helpful:

◆ Why do you want to recommit to your partner?
◆ Has the nature of your commitment changed? How?
◆ What commitments did you originally make to each other?
◆ What commitments have remained the same?

◆ What commitments have changed?

◆ Are there additional commitments you would like to make to each other?

◆ Do you wish to include your children in your recommitment?

A recommitment ritual can be a beautiful way to say to your partner that you would commit to her/him all over again, that the love you feel has matured and expanded over the years. A magical recommitment ceremony honoring your relationship can be a powerful way to celebrate your bond.

11

Optional Activities

These optional activities may enhance your handfasting.

Invitations

Some couples enjoy sending printed invitations to family and friends, while others write a simple note, email or call prospective guests on the telephone. Any choice you make in this area that fits your budget is appropriate.

Over the years many conventions have arisen about the "correct" format and style for printed invitations. If you are having your invitations done professionally, it is likely the printer will know how invitations are commonly arranged, spelled and worded. Invitations can be engraved, and your printer can help you determine which of many possible choices best suits your needs.

Customarily, the size of an invitation is 7½" by 5½" and it is printed on the first page of a doubled sheet of paper. Formal invitations come with two envelopes. The inside envelope is not gummed and is not meant to be sealed. The invitation is placed inside this ungummed envelope, which is placed inside the outer envelope so that the flap faces up. If your printer has included a piece of tissue paper, it should be left in place.

Keep in mind:

◆ Order invitations several months in advance. Make certain before you order that you know all the particulars (time, date, location).

◆ If possible, get as many envelopes and invitations as you need at one time. Not only will re-ordering cost more, there can also be variations in paper production that will cause a mismatch between the new items and what remains from your previous order.

◆ Read and reread your order before you commit to it. If a mistake is yours, in all likelihood the printer will not correct it unless you pay the cost.

◆ Plan to mail invitations approximately six weeks before your handfasting or even sooner for out-of-town guests. The minimum time before your ceremony for mailing invitations is two weeks. Remember, it will take time to put together your address list and address the envelopes, so leave plenty of time to prepare your invitations before they must be mailed.

◆ Create or ask an attendant to create a system to keep track of replies. This can be done with your computer, a checklist or index cards.

Guest Lists

Whether you are planning to send printed invitations or not, you will need a guest list to give you an idea of how many people to expect at your handfasting and the reception. You and your part-ner-to-be may create your lists separately or together, but if you do this individually, start developing your combined list by removing any duplicates. Generally, expect 75 percent to 80 percent response to your invitations.

If the size of your handfasting is an issue, consider inviting some guests only to the reception and not to the ceremony or vice versa. It is always important to keep track of whom you invite to what. If you need an accurate count because of space concerns, you may find it necessary to contact those who did not respond to ask if they plan on coming.

Addresses on formal invitations are traditionally hand-written in black ink. The only abbreviations considered appropriate for use on envelopes are Mrs., Ms., Mr. and Jr. The names of cities and states as well as street addresses are written out (e.g., 125 Elm Street, Omaha, Nebraska). If you are inviting a family, the adults' names are written on the outside envelope, and both the adults' and the children's names are written on the inside envelope. Unpartnered adults should receive their own invitation, and the space available may determine whether or not you allow them to bring a guest. Return addresses can be embossed on the envelope flap or address stickers may be placed in the envelope's upper left-hand corner.

Some example invitations follow.

Examples of Invitations

Formal

Mr. and Dr. Kendall Stromb
request the honor of
your presence
at the (handfasting, union or marriage) of their daughter

Melissa Jane
to
Stephen Allen Black

on Friday, the thirteenth of November
Two thousand and two
at two o'clock p.m.
Cleveland Community Center
Cleveland, Ohio

reception to follow.
r.s.v.p.
Dr. Kendall Stromb
216-847-8317

There are other ways a formal invitation can be issued. If someone other than your parents is issuing the invitation or if your parents
are divorced, your printer or your local library has information about
the appropriate wording.

Informal

Dear Ffiona,
Bill and Nicholas are being handfasted at the grove in Cherokee
Park, Sunday, May 23rd, at 2:30. We hope you will be able to join
us and can return to the house afterward for a reception.

Sincerely,
Wendy

Open Circle Invitation

An open circle invitation is issued to every member of your circle, nest, grove, coven, meeting or other spiritual group. This invitation can be announced by you, your group's Priest/ess or can be printed in any publication of the group.

Wedding/Engagement Announcements

You may want to announce your handfasting in local newspapers. Depending on the part of the country, these may be called either wedding or engagement announcements. Virtually all newspapers print announcements of heterosexual engagements, and the number of newspapers that print them for lesbian and gay couples is steadily increasing. Check your local newspaper for their policy, and if they do not publish these announcements for single-sex couples, you can always ask anyway. You may be the first.

Daily Papers

Generally, information forms for announcements can be picked up at the newspaper office. Photos often accompany announcements, and you may want to have a handfasting portrait taken for this purpose. Announcements are generally published during the month of the handfasting. In some areas, the announcement appears on the day of your handfasting.

Weekly Papers

Small weekly papers are usually more informal and may or may not have forms for you to complete. They might provide more intimate coverage, accept an article you have written yourself or assign a staff writer to interview you.

Photography/Videography

Many Priest/esses stipulate that photos or videos may not be taken during the ceremony, so check in advance. Some Priest/esses allow inconspicuous video or standard photography if there are no lights or flashes used. Be sure to share your decisions and the Priest/ess' preference with your family and friends who may want to take pictures.

Tips and Trivia: Photography
◆ Today, many couples choose candid photography rather than or in addition to a formal, traditional wedding portfolio.

Money-Saving Alternatives: Photography
◆ Hire a professional photographer for your handfasting and ask a friend or family member to take candid shots.
◆ Check at local trade schools for a photography student who may be interested in taking pictures of your handfasting and then turning the film over to you for developing.
◆ Hire a photographer only for an hour, not for the entire function.
◆ Have several amateurs videotape your handfasting and reception. Take the best of each and edit them together.
◆ Give disposable cameras to guests and ask them to take

photos and leave the cameras with you (or an attend-ant) after the reception. You'll end up with different people's perspectives of your ceremony.

Gifts

For couples just setting up housekeeping, a wonderful benefit of having a public joining ceremony can be the gifts from family and friends. A gift registry is a free service provided by department stores, jewelry stores, travel agencies and gift shops. When you register, be prepared to answer questions about your household needs — not only the type of silver and china you would like, but also your preference for sheets, towels and any color schemes you plan for your home. If you are going to complete your registration with your partner-to-be, shopping beforehand and agreeing on items can be helpful.

Registry experts suggest registering for a few expensive gifts, since groups of people often go together to purchase a gift.

The registry keeps track of each gift purchased and lets subsequent shoppers know what has already been bought from your list. You can sign up with a gift registry as soon as your ceremony date is certain and you have an idea of the items you want.

Keep track of who gave you which gift so that you can write thank-you notes. Some couples have a "gift attendant" who keeps track of gifts at the reception and showers. Others simply ask someone to make a note of who sent which gift as they open them.

Children

Handfasting couples, especially those with children, often have a playroom for young people who come to the ceremony and/or reception. This involves making arrangements for an appropriate person/s to watch the children and help entertain them. The playroom is best when filled with toys, games and/or a television and videos.

The Reception

If the place where you have your handfasting has a large room, it may be a natural spot for your reception. If not, many couples host outdoor receptions in parks or even in their backyards. Halls for receptions may be rented from hotels, country clubs, university student unions and restaurants, American Legions, Veterans of Foreign Wars, service organizations and ethnic clubs. To avoid problems, make certain before you rent a location that the managers are comfortable with Pagans using their facility.

Receptions typically feature food and some type of entertainment. What is served and the kind of entertainment vary in different areas and from couple to couple.

Tips and Trivia: Reception Decoration

◆ You can make it easy for your guests to leave congratulations cards for you by providing attractively decorated baskets around the reception area.

Additional Questions about Reception Sites

◆ Is the site beautiful, and does its energy feel good?

◆ Is the site available on the day and time you want?

◆ Are there any other activities scheduled there on the same day? If so, at what time? Is there plenty of time between that activity and yours?

◆ Will noise carry from one room to another? Have any arrangements been made for soundproofing? Do they work?

◆ Will the site's staff set up the room for you? If so, when will it be ready?

◆ Is this space large enough that your guests will be comfortable and all your activities can be accommodated?

◆ Is there a dance floor? Is it large enough to accommodate the number of guests you are inviting? If there isn't one, can you rent one and have it installed?

◆ Are chairs, tables or linens provided along with the rental?

◆ Will the lighting adapt to your needs?

◆ Are the acoustics good for the activities planned?

◆ Have safety precautions been taken? For example, are there fire exits, extinguishers, exit signs?

◆ Is this site accessible to people with disabilities?

◆ Are the bathrooms in good working condition? Are they clean and well maintained?

◆ Is there enough parking for your guests, or are there other places to park nearby?

◆ Is there a coatroom or a place to hang coats?

◆ If you want to serve alcohol, does the facility have a liquor license?

◆ What is the smoking policy? Is there a designated smoking area?

◆ Does the facility maintain insurance? Will it cover you and your activities?

◆ Is this a place that should have a license from a Department of Health? Do they hold such a license?

Tips and Trivia: Reception Food

◆ Food and drinks for the reception are usually the biggest expense of a handfasting.

◆ Our current version of the wedding cake came from the French who piled up wedding cookies and put icing on them.

◆ In Celtic culture, every handfasting guest received a

wedding cookie. Any cookies remaining were shared with the entire village.

◆ Wedding cookies ensured a couple's fertility. Each member of a handfasting couple had a bite of the cookie and the rest was broken over the bride's head. Those attending the handfasting scrambled for cookie pieces, believing that any person who ate some of it would share the luck of the handfasting couple. There were periods in Rome when, if a cookie was not broken over the head of the bride, the marriage was not considered legal.

Money-Saving Alternatives: Reception Ideas

◆ Make your own ice sculpture with a do-it-yourself mold purchased from a catering supply store.

◆ Ask a friend or relative who is a good cook to make some or all of the food. You can still make the presentation elegant with skirted tables and expensive-looking tablecloths.

◆ Have a cappuccino and espresso bar in place of alcohol.

◆ In any area of your handfasting, from flowers to formal wear or cake to catering, shop around to compare. You may find a wide difference in prices for the same service or item.

Things to Consider when Planning a Reception

◆ Do you have a theme?

◆ Other than your attendants, do you want additional host/esses?

◆ Will your reception be staffed by professionals (for example, if you are renting a hotel), or will you need to recruit volunteers to take care of the activities?

◆ Will there be food? What is the menu?

◆ Will there be beverages? What will you serve?

◆ Will there be entertainment? What kind?

◆ Will there be music? What types of music do you want, and what selections will be played?

◆ Will you need any supplies or equipment? Where will they come from? Will you need to purchase or rent any of these items? How will they get to the reception?

◆ Do you want to have a guest book? Who will be responsible for it?

◆ Will you have a receiving line? What will be the order in which people will stand to receive the guests?

◆ Do you intend to dance? Who will provide the music, what type of music will there be and in what order?

◆ Will there be toasts? Do you need to talk to someone to make certain this will happen?

◆ Will there be a cake? Where will it come from, and how will it get to the reception? Who will serve it and on what? (Does the site provide plates, etc., or do you need to bring these items?)

◆ Will you or any of your guests sit down formally to eat? What are the seating arrangements?

◆ Do you want to have favors for your guests? What will they be and when will they be given out?

◆ Will there be a garter and bouquet toss? When and where will this happen?

◆ Do you need to make arrangements for clean-up? Who will do this?

Money-Saving Alternatives: Handfasting Favors

◆ Inexpensive handfasting favor 1: Give each guest a variety of seeds or a tiny tree with a note saying that as these grow, so will the joy you shared at your handfasting.

◆ Inexpensive handfasting favor 2: Make individual scrolls on parchment with a message for each guest. Roll each scroll, tie it with a ribbon and present them to your guests.

Tips and Trivia: Receiving Lines

◆ Allow thirty to forty minutes for every 200 guests to pass through a receiving line. (If fewer or more than 200 guests, plan proportionally.)

Food

Unless your family or friends prepare the food, your best option is probably a caterer. Assuming you have time to make food for your own reception is, in all likelihood, a mistake. The emotional, physical and spiritual preparation are quite enough without the additional responsibility of preparing food for your guests.

For many couples, their handfasting would not be complete without a tiered cake topped with miniature figures. The traditional toppers for a wedding cake of a plastic bride and groom are no longer the only option. You can have something that represents an interest you and your partner share, such as a set of teddy bears, a miniature set of motorcycles or a tiny pair of Irish setters. More elegant options are wine glasses filled with flowers, a mirror with a small basket full of candy kisses or some alternative figurines available at a local gift store.

For same-sex couples who want small figures of a couple on top of the cake, miniatures of two men or two women are now available at many gift shops which cater to gay and lesbian shoppers or via the internet.

Money-Saving Alternatives: Cakes

◆ Decorate the top of your cake with fresh flowers from your local grocery or wholesale florist.

◆ If you would like to have a larger cake than you can afford, ask your baker to make the bottom layers out of Styrofoam These can be easily iced over, giving the impression of a tall cake at a much smaller price.

Cutting the Cake

Cutting the handfasting cake can be a ceremony in and of itself, involving lights, music and great fun. If you are having a sit-down meal, the traditional time to cut the cake is when the meal is finished. This way, the cake becomes the desert for the meal. If you plan to serve a luncheon or buffet, the cake is generally cut and served towards the end of the reception.

Traditionally, the last thing done at a reception is to toss the bouquet and garter. Cutting the cake takes place immediately before this and includes enough time for the guests to eat their cake before the tosses.

Cake cutting, particularly of a multilayer cake, is an art. If your caterer does not provide this service, make certain whomever you ask to perform this task knows how to best accomplish it.

Many couples bring their own cake-cutting knife and a server, sometimes festooned with flowers or decorated to match any theme. Some couples honor their parents or grandparents by using the same utensils that they used for their wedding cake. One word of caution: Many wedding experts say that one of the most commonly forgotten items is the cake-cutting knife and server.

Tips and Trivia: Wedding Cakes

◆ Newlyweds customarily cut their wedding cake hand-over-hand and then each feed the other a bite of cake. The parents of the handfasting couple are usually served their cake before the rest of the guests.

◆ Traditionally, it is believed you can draw dreams of your future partner by placing a piece of wedding cake under your pillow. In some areas this custom was facilitated by a special cake called a groom's cake. Unlike the standard white wedding cake, a groom's cake is generally a chocolate cake or a fruitcake. The groom's cake can be precut into small squares and packaged in small gold or white boxes or wrapped in shiny paper and tied with a ribbon. In some areas of Europe, a groom's cake is a common gift for the couple from the groom's relatives, who also take responsibility for packaging the pieces. Some couples prefer to serve the groom's cake as an alternative treat at the reception. Boxes can be provided so the guests can package their own cake to take home.

◆ A ribbon pull is another divinatory custom. When the cake is iced, a variety of charms, each with a ribbon attached, is hidden between the layers. Charms could include four-leaf clover or a horseshoe for luck, a heart for love or a ring for marriage. Attendants gather round the cake and each pulls out a ribbon for a charm that will tell them their future.

Tips and Trivia: The Wedding Toast

◆ After the handfasting couple has been served, the best man or honor attendant traditionally proposes the first toast. This is usually followed by toasts from other relatives, friends or even the handfasting couple.

◆ Everything at a reception is considered optional except the toast to the new couple. If you will not serve alcohol at your reception, consider having a non-alcoholic sparkling wine or champagne.

◆ In some European countries, it is a custom for the handfasting couple to "plight their troth" with a wedding cup. If the reception is a sit-down dinner, a wedding cup is placed at the head table; at a less formal occasion, it is placed on the same table as the cake. The handfasting couple drinks their first toast from this cup. There are two common types of handfasting cups. One is a silver cup in the shape of a woman who is holding another cup over her head. The handfasting couple drinks from this cup at the same time. A second type of cup looks like a small bowl standing on a pedestal. Each handfaster drinks from this cup individually.

Money-Saving Alternatives: Reception Options

◆ Use bottles of champagne that you will serve later as part of your decorations. Tie flowers, ribbons or other ornaments to the necks of the bottles for a festive flair.

◆ Discount grocery and food warehouses sell sparkling wine by the case. You can serve this instead of or along with champagne for considerable savings.

◆ See if you can borrow the silver and china for your reception from friends or family.

◆ Hire a student from a near-by chef's or vocational school (food preparation program) to cater your reception.

◆ Have two different receptions: one that immediately follows the ceremony at which you serve cake and a few small snack items, and another, expanded reception later or on another day.

◆ Create your own dance music by making tapes or burning CDs, and rent a sound system from a local rental store. Ask a friend or family member to DJ.

◆ Use large books, pots or even heavy boxes filled with bricks to create a back-to-front tiered presentation of the food. Cover each of these makeshift food-service shelves with tablecloths or napkins that match the rest of your decorations.

Caterers offer an extensive range of services and foods for indoor or outdoor receptions. In most areas, any level of catering — formal sit-down dinners, elegant buffets, simple appetizers or just deserts — is available. If you are from an area that has traditional regional cuisine or if you have a theme for your handfasting, consider these possibilities for reception fare. You could serve mead if your handfasting has a Renaissance theme, or consider a clam-bake if you are planning a beach-side handfasting or if this is something for which your region is famous. How much and what type of food you serve is up to you.

Tips and Trivia: Leftovers

◆ Many people arrange to have leftover food from their reception donated to local food kitchens or homeless shelters.

Entertainment

The entertainment will directly affect the way you and your guests celebrate at your reception. Your reception may be one of the largest parties you will ever host, and there are many entertainment possibilities.

Some couples have the same musicians perform at both their handfasting and their reception, while others have different performers. If you are planning to pose for pictures between the ceremony and reception, consider providing music to entertain your guests until you can arrive.

Many receptions feature dancing. If you plan to dance, make certain the site has enough room and enough electrical outlets and power to accommodate your entertainers. Also, check to see that your space has a dance floor or make plans to rent one that can be installed before your reception.

Tips and Trivia: The Traditional
Order of Dances at a Reception
◆ The handfasting couple dances with each other. The father of the bride cuts in on the groom and the groom moves to dance with his new mother-in-law. The bride then dances with the-groom's father, and the groom dances with his mother. Each primary attendant dances with the member of the couple whom s/he did not stand up with. All other guests are then invited to join in. At some time during the reception, each member of the handfasting couple dances with each of the attendants.

◆ This same type of order can be followed at a same-sex handfasting reception. The couple dances first, and at some point a parent of each member cuts in and dances with their new son- or daughter-by-handfasting. The rest of the order can follow as above.

Dance music can be provided in a variety of ways ranging from a live band to a disc jockey. What type of music will you and your guests enjoy? You can have anything from big band to rock to polka. After deciding on the type of music, look for entertainers who specialize in that style. Check on their fees and availability. (Many performers book their dates up to a year in advance.)

Before hiring them, you may want to meet with and audition musicians or disc jockeys. Some musicians will give you a cassette or videotape of their music, while others will direct you to times and locations of a performance you can attend.

There are, of course, other types of entertainment that you might choose for your reception. Among these are:

◆ Carriage rides
◆ Release of live butterflies
◆ Card party
◆ Activities for children
◆ Throwing confetti or some

other earth-friendly, festive materials at the happy couple, usually as
they leave the reception
    ◆ Blowing bubbles
        ◆ Karaoke
            ◆ Musical performances
                ◆ Reception lines (At one time, formal weddings
    always included a receiving line, but many couples now
    forego this, no matter how formal the ceremony.)
                ◆ Games, such as the television game show, The
    Newlywed Game.
                ◆ Dollar dances, where people pin dollar bills on
    the bride in exchange for a dance

        The entertainment for your handfasting is entirely
up to you and your partner. However, be certain to make choices
that you will remember with pleasure and joy.

Tips and Trivia: Reception Customs

    ◆ Throwing the garter removed from the bride's leg to a
group of bachelors is a traditional heterosexual wedding reception activity. The bachelor who catches the garter is believed to
be the next groom.
    ◆ The bride traditionally tosses her bouquet over her shoul-
der to a waiting group of single women. She who catches the
bouquet is next to be married.
    ◆ In Rome, candy and nuts were tossed at newlyweds.
    ◆ By custom, showering a new couple with rice or grain was
believed to ensure both their fertility and their protection; however, rice or grains left on the ground will be eaten by birds and

can make them sick or even die. Most contemporary couples substitute earth-friendly items.

◆ Tying strings of empty tin cans to the back of the newlyweds' vehicle discourages misguided spirits from accompanying them.

◆ Couples leaving on a trip were at one time showered with shoes by their friends for luck and fertility. People believed that part of the friends' souls was transferred to the soles of their shoes. Tossing shoes conveyed good luck to both the tossers and to the new couple. This custom has all but faded, but the newer custom of tying old shoes to the newlyweds' car bumper is a remnant of this belief.

◆ The places in between.... the hinge places were the locus of significant power in Celtic cultures. For newlyweds to cross over the threshold of their home individually was considered unlucky, and so the tradition developed of the groom carrying the bride over the threshold. Depending on the country, stepping directly on the threshold can bring either good luck or bad.

Things That Need to be Done after the Reception

◆ The space where the ceremony and the reception were held need to be cleaned to whatever specifications you have agreed. In most cases, this includes removing all decorations, flowers and any other items that you brought into the space. Unless you ask beforehand, do not assume that leaving food, flowers or any other items will be acceptable to those who rented you the space. If the site does not provide clean-up services, remember to make arrangements with family, friends or someone else to tidy the space.

◆ Arrange for someone to collect all personal items which were brought into the space and transport them to a pre-assigned place, such as the home of a parent, friend or that of the hand-fasting couple. Reclaim the items that you brought for your service and reception and special mementoes from the events. These might include the top layer of the cake, the decoration from the top of the cake, flowers, the unity candle, gifts which were brought to the handfasting or reception, the guest book, any leftover programs or favors and any lost items left by guests.

◆ If you get dressed at the handfasting site or will change clothes before you leave the reception, designate someone to gather clothing that you or your attendants leave behind and pick up luggage, make up, hair dryers or other things that may have been part of the dressing process. Tell this designated person where to take these items and where to put them within that space. If you or your partner has worn a gown, be sure to provide specific instructions about what you want done with it. Some people want their gown to go directly to a dry cleaner for cleaning and preparation for storage, while others simply take it home.

◆ One of the traditional responsibilities of a primary attendant is to return any rental clothing or equipment.

◆ Pay all staff or participants who need to be reimbursed, such as musicians or your caterer. Have checks or cash ready and labeled, in different envelopes for each person. Designate someone to distribute them.

◆ Make arrangements for any leftover food or drinks. You may be billed for unused items in your order, so you may want to take these items with you, including unopened bottles of champagne or wine or food.

◆ Assign someone to thank the staff and volunteers who helped create your handfasting. Although you will want to express your appreciation personally, it is wise to ask someone officially to perform this function so that in the excitement no one is left out and feelings are not hurt. You can ask this person to say something like, "Susan asked me to be sure to thank you for your beautiful solo today."

◆ Pick a designated driver in case some of your guests get overly festive with the toasts.

Money-Saving Alternatives: Transportation
◆ Find someone with a collector car (convertible Cadillac, 1901 Oldsmobile or any other interesting vehicle) who can transport you and your and your partner to the handfasting.

Tips and Trivia: Limousine Service
◆ If you are looking for quality in a limousine service, call a local five-star hotel and ask the concierge for the name of the service they hire for their best guests.

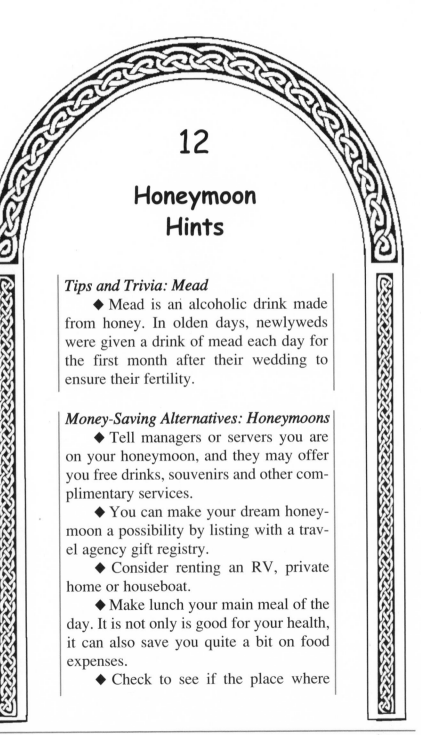

12

Honeymoon Hints

Tips and Trivia: Mead

◆ Mead is an alcoholic drink made from honey. In olden days, newlyweds were given a drink of mead each day for the first month after their wedding to ensure their fertility.

Money-Saving Alternatives: Honeymoons

◆ Tell managers or servers you are on your honeymoon, and they may offer you free drinks, souvenirs and other complimentary services.

◆ You can make your dream honeymoon a possibility by listing with a travel agency gift registry.

◆ Consider renting an RV, private home or houseboat.

◆ Make lunch your main meal of the day. It is not only is good for your health, it can also save you quite a bit on food expenses.

◆ Check to see if the place where

you are staying offers free appetizers during happy hour. For the price of a drink, you could have a light dinner for free.

◆ Look for places to stay where breakfast is included.

◆ If you are honeymooning in another country, exchange money at a bank instead of at your hotel or an airport for a significant savings.

◆ Take items such as film, sunscreen and shampoo with you. These items are often much more expensive in tourist destinations.

◆ For economical dining options, ask taxi drivers, store clerks or any other locals for their favorite inexpensive places to eat.

◆ Bring drinks and snacks back with you to your room so you won't be tempted by the expensive items in the mini-bar.

◆ Find out if there is a per-call charge for phoning from your room. You may find it more economical to use your cell phone or find a nearby pay phone.

◆ Ask if your hotel has a shuttle or if they provide any other free transportation, and take advantage of it whenever possible.

◆ Fill your honeymoon with romantic inexpensive or free activities, such as taking walks, watching the sunset or visiting a local park or garden.

13

Taking It Apart

Divorce or Estrangement

The act of joining a couple's hands at a handfasting provides one of the most basic philosophical differences between this and a conventional marriage ceremony. In the past, couples were joined together in perpetuity with no possibility for release. Until recently, marriage was viewed as a lifelong commitment which was irrevocable, regardless of the actions of a partner or the incompatibility of the couple. A wedding ceremony locked two people together for a lifetime in accordance with the will of God and the church. Breaking this holy bond sanctioned by God and church did (and in some cases still does) have severe consequences. (For example, Catholics who divorce are not allowed to take communion.)

Although a handfasting is viewed as a lasting commitment, it only remains as long as the couple chooses. Because magic is

used to bond the handfasting couple, it is important to have a way
to release the magic should it become necessary.

The energy of the ritual is held in the knot tied by the
Priest/ess during the ceremony. Most of us hope that our commitment to our partner will last a lifetime. However, if a couple de-
velops conflicts that cannot be reconciled, either person can untie
the knot or, when in agreement, the couple can untie the knot
together. This releases the energy of the ritual and frees the magic
that was used to unite them.

(If a marriage license was involved, the couple will also have to
petition the court for a divorce.)

Death

The death of a handfasted partner can be a heartbreaking experience. Everyone whose partner dies will have some similar issues.
These can include the grief of losing a partner, dealing with estate
and money matters, a change in social position and many other
experiences both large and small.

For those who lose a handfasted partner, other issues arise. If
you included the tying of hands in your ceremony, there is the question of what to do with the knot that was tied. The surviving partner may want to untie the knot as a step in her/his grieving process
or when s/he wants to enter another committed relationship. Each
individual's decision is extremely personal. Although many actions
are possible, some options are:

◆ Untie half of the knot.

◆ Do not untie the knot, but burn it to release the energy.

◆ Throw the cord in moving water.

◆ Bury the cord or place it in the coffin with the deceased
partner.

Appendices

Appendix A: The Ceremony: Several Options

Appendix B: Potential Timeline

Appendix C: Budget / Finances

Appendix D: Who Traditionally Pays for What

Appendix E: A Checklist

Appendix F: Legal Credentials

Appendix G: Creating Vows

Appendix A:
The Ceremony: Several Options

Following are rituals that have been used by handfasting couples. The pronouns in each ceremony depend on the sex of the people being handfasted.

Simple Handfasting
The guests are seated.

Casting the Circle
The Priest/ess casts the circle by walking the perimeter. Four attendants follow, each with one of the elements. When all have walked around the circle, the Priest/ess begins.

Welcome and Intentions
Priest/ess: Honored guests, we welcome you to this gathering, the union of (name) and (name). We have come here today to witness the commitment of these two people as they make vows to one another. We ask the company here assembled to join in this celebration of their dedication and pledge to one another.

The Priest/ess moves to the East, and the East attendant lights incense.

Priest/ess: We call the element of air — the breath which connects us all, that this union may have wisdom and clear communication.

The Priest/ess moves to the South, and the South attendant lights her candle.

Priest/ess: We call the element of fire — the passion which cleanses and purifies, that this union may have integrity.

The Priest/ess moves to the West, and the West attendant pours wine into the chalice.

Priest/ess: We call the element of water — the fluid which teaches us love and compassion, that this union may have empathy and tenderness.

The Priest/ess moves to the North, and the North attendant places bread on her altar.

Priest/ess: We call the element of earth — the stability of the land, that this union may have endurance and stamina.

The Priest/ess moves to the Center and invokes the Goddess.

Priest/ess: We call on the Great Goddess, the Mother of us all, she who calls us to evoke her with our love. It is in loving one another that we find her.

Exchanging Vows

The Priest/ess and the couple move to the East.

Priest/ess: At this time, (name) and (name) will exchange their vows. These are the promises they make to one another, witnessed and affirmed by each of you.

The handfasting couple reads or recites the vows that they have prepared.

Lighting the Unity Candle

The Priest/ess and the couple move to the South. The South attendant hands each handfaster a candle and lights them.

Priest/ess: Fire brings us warmth, passion and illumination. As each woman lights her own candle, she fills it with her own essence.

The handfasting couple lights the Unity Candle.

Priest/ess: As they light the Unity Candle, their spirits are joined together. And our lives are made brighter by their love.

Sharing Wine

The Priest/ess and the couple move to the West. The West attendant hands the chalice to handfaster 1.

Handfaster 1: May you always know compassion, tenderness and fulfillment, and may I be their instrument.

Handfaster 1 holds the chalice to the lips of handfaster 2, who drinks from it.

Handfaster 2 : May you always know compassion, tenderness and fulfillment, and may I be their instrument.

Handfaster 2 holds the chalice to the lips of handfaster 1, who drinks from it.

Sharing Bread

The Priest/ess and the couple move to the North. The North attendant hands bread to handfaster 1.

Handfaster 1: May the bounty of the earth be with us as we travel life's journey together.

Handfaster 1 feeds bread to handfaster 2.

Handfaster 2: May the bounty of the earth be with us as we travel life's journey together.

Handfaster 2 feeds bread to handfaster 1.

Exchanging Rings and Tying the Cord

The Priest/ess and the couple move to the Center.

Priest/ess: The ring is a circle, a symbol of the eternal cycles of love and nature. It is a visual and constant reminder of the bond between these two.

The couple exchanges rings. The Priest/ess picks up the cord and addresses the guests.

Priest/ess: I ask each of you to focus on this cord. With it, (name) and (name) will be bound together. Concentrate your energy on this cord. Invest it with your hopes for this couple, with desires for their happiness and wishes for their health and prosperity.

The Priest/ess holds the cord up until she feels the energy is right, then s/he wraps the cord around the hands of the couple and ties it with a knot. Each attendant releases her element in her own way, and the Priest/ess releases Center.

Presentation

Priest/ess: Before this company assembled, (name) and (name) are bound together for as long as their love shall last. By your measure be ye bound, by your hearts be ye free. You are now united.

The handfasted couple leaves the circle followed by the attendants.

A Handfasting Ceremony for
Couples Who Include Their Children

Prelude: Piano Selections (Various Composers)

Vocal Selection: *Reality, Peace I Ask of Thee, Oh River* (Traditional)

Processional: *Pachelbel's Canon in D*

Vocal Selection: *How Can I Keep From Singing?* (Traditional) Choir

Greeting and Gathering

Priest/ess: Today, family and friends have gathered here to celebrate the relationship of (name) and (name). At this time I extend to (name) and (name)'s family and friends their greetings and express their appreciation for your sharing this blessed event with them. To the honored guests of the East, they welcome you and ask that you share the beginning of this union. To the honored guests of the South, please share today the warmth and power of their friendship. Honored guests of the West, please hold in your hearts the spirit of emotion which surrounds every marriage, for today especially, love and joy. And honored guests of the North, I invite you to surround these two and their children with the love and stability that create a home.

I welcome (name) and (name) into this circle of beloved friends and family and ask that the spirit of love be here with us today. May the blessings of the Goddess be here with us today.

Narrator: Traditions help bring people together to form a common bond. They reinforce family and friendships.

Traditions are also an excellent launching pad for communication, and since (name) and (name) both have strong feelings about the importance of good communication, it is fitting that I, the Narrator, communicate the various traditions in their ceremony. It is their hope that these explanations will help answer some questions you may have, thereby promoting understanding and good communication.

Many of the traditions (name) and (name) are using in their ceremony are found in different cultures, and all are found in the Irish or Celtic countries-(name)'s primary background.

Therefore, whenever you hear the bell ring (a prime symbol of communication), I will explain the tradition that is about to take place.

Declaration of Family

Priest/ess: This is the union of an entire family. This is not just two people joining together in marriage, but two people who have chosen to create a family. I welcome their children into this ceremony: (children's names).

Vocal Selection: *How Could Anyone Ever Tell You?* (Libby Roderick) Choir

Presentation of the Chalice

Narrator: The chalice is the symbol of the universe, as is the womb. It is a reminder that we all start the cycle of life in our mother's wombs. To drink from the chalice is to honor all beginnings and to proclaim that to live well, you must not be afraid to taste life. By drinking from this chalice, (name) and (name) proclaim they are ready to taste life together no matter what the universe may pour into their cup.

Priest/ess: Blessed are the waters of the earth, which sustain us and give us life. Today, (name) and (name) drink from this chalice. May your life together be based on good communication. May you also drink deeply the pleasures of life, sweet and full of love. May you be surrounded by the emotional well-being of friends and family.

Exchange of Vows

Narrator: (Name) and (name) have written vows to share with each other.

Priest/ess: Please face one another. (Name), will you begin?

The couple exchanges vows.

Exchange of Rings and Blessing

Priest/ess: Rings have long been a token of love. They are circles with no beginning or ending. They represent eternity and on-going growth, as well as long-lasting love.

Priest/ess: (Name), do you take this ring with love and devotion?

Handfaster 1: (Name), with this ring, I take you to be my wife, partner and friend.

Priest/ess: (Name), do you take this ring with love and devotion?

Handfaster 2: (Name), with this ring I take you to be my wife, partner and friend.

Priest/ess: Gratitude to Mother Earth, sailing through night and day — and to Her soil: rich, rare and sweet. In our minds, so be it.

Gratitude to Plants, the sun-facing, light-changing leaves and fine root-hairs, standing still through wind and rain. Their dance is in the flowing spiral grain. In our minds, so be it.

Gratitude to Air, bearing the soaring swift and silent owl at dawn. Breath of our song, clear spirit breeze. In our minds, so be it.

Gratitude to Wild Beings, our sisters, teaching secrets, freedom and ways, who share with us their wisdom. In our minds, so be it.

Gratitude to Water: clouds, lakes, rivers, glacier; holding or releasing, streaming through all. In our minds, so be it.

Gratitude to the Sun: blinding, pulsing light through trunks of trees, through mists, warming caves where bears and snakes sleep; she who wakes us. In our minds, so be it.

Gratitude to the Great Sky, who holds billions of stars-and beyond that, beyond all powers — and yet is also within us. In our minds, so be it.

Lighting the Unity Candle

Narrator: The candle is a symbol of knowledge and growth. The Unity Candle is the symbol of learning about each other and growing together. (Name) and (name) will join (children's names) and they will all light the candle together.

Priest/ess: May the light of the Goddess always be in your hearts. May the transformation in your life bring enlightenment.

Instrumental Selection: *Moonlight Sonata* (Beethoven)

Vocal Selection: *Give Yourself to Love* (Kate Wolf) Choir

Jumping the Broom

Narrator: The broom is a symbol of change. Jumping the broom represents leaving behind one life while jumping into another. It also promotes luck as the first task (name) and (name) will do together as wife and wife.

The broom is placed on the floor or held at a comfortable height. The couple holds hands and jumps over the broom.

Introduction and Presentation of the New Family

Priest/ess: Today, witnessed by friends and family, I present (name) and (name), united as a couple. Also witnessed today, this couple has formed a family. I present to you the entire family.

May the spirit of the Goddess be always with them. Honored guests of North, West, South and East, please open this circle of family and friends.

Welcome (name), (name) and (children's names) into their new life.

Recessional: *Purcell's Trumpet Voluntary* (Jeremiah Clarke)

The handfasted couple and their children leave the circle, followed by the attendants.

Handfasting Ceremony which Honors the Goddess and God

This ceremony can be performed by one or two Priest/esses.

The guests are called together by the Priest/esses and asked to stand in a circle.

Attunement

Priest/ess 1: As we enter into sacred space for this ceremony, let each of us pause and remember those we love. There are many different types of love: the love of a mother for a child, the love of a brother for a brother, the love of a friend or the love *of one heart for another. We come here today to recognize the love of one person for another; a love so strong, so enduring, that it cannot help but be proclaimed and celebrated.*

Casting the Circle

The Circle is cast by the Priest/esses. This includes a purification using the four elements (earth, air, fire and water). An opening is cut for the couple to enter, either by one of the Priest/esses or by a designated Guardian in the North. The Maiden brings the attendants into the circle and leads them to their positions. She returns for the handfasting couple, and the circle is closed again.

Statement of Intention

Priest/ess 2: (Name) *and* (name) *have asked each of you here today to witness and recognize, to consecrate and honor, their love and commitment. They have found their love for one another to be so strong that each of them has chosen to declare and affirm it to their family, friends and community and to ask your assistance in acknowledging and formalizing the bond between them. It is a bond founded in love, in passion, in honesty and in understanding. Building on the strengths of their past and honoring their present, they are here today to state their intention to unite their futures and to bring together their physical, emotional, mental and spiritual lives.*

Priest/ess 1 (turning toward the couple): *It is in relationship with others that we learn the most about ourselves. Life on the earth is not meant to be filled with sorrow and struggle. It is meant to be filled with joy. We are meant to honor and celebrate love wherever we find it. It is said that when we pass into the other realm, one of the two questions the Great Goddess will ask us about our life is, "Have you loved enough?" May* (name) *and* (name) be able to answer her question with sincerity because they both loved and were loved.

Invocations

Priest/ess 2: Let us now call the Great Mother, asking her to be present as we consecrate and celebrate this union.

Mother, You Hold Me in the Palm of Your Hand is sung as an invocation to the Goddess.

Priest/ess 1: We call forth the consort of the Great Mother, the horned one, the green man, the year king, asking him to be present as we consecrate and celebrate this union.

Pan, Woden, Bothomay chant is sung as an invocation to the God.

The handfasting couple stands and is purified with incense.

Handfasting

Priest/ess 2: (Name), do you come here to be joined in the presence of the Goddess according to your own free will and anticipating the greatest good from this union?

Handfaster 1: I am here of my own free will, and I choose this union.

Priest/ess 1: (Name), do you come here to be joined in the presence of the God according to your own free will and anticipating the greatest good from this union?

Handfaster 2: I am here of my own free will, and I choose this union.

Priest/ess 2: Then let us begin the fastening of hands. (Name) and (name) have asked each of you here today to assist with a magical affirmation of their relationship. You are not only witnesses to, but also participants in, raising the energy which will sustain this union. From this time onward, (name) and (name) will be recognized among family and friends, community and cosmos, as a couple.

Priest/ess 2 (picks up cord): *I ask you now to join with (name) and (name) and focus on this cord, investing it with the energy of the joy of two people's love, the pleasure of simple things shared, the satisfaction of becoming family, the pleasure of watching each other mature, the strength to persevere through difficulties, and passion enough to last a lifetime.*

Priest/ess 2 holds the cord up while the guests invest it with energy. When Priest/ess 2 feels the energy to be at its peak, she motions for the couple to join hands and fastens the cord around their wrists.

Priest/ess 2: The hopes and wishes of those you have chosen to share this ritual, along with your own, are now invested in this cord. I join your hands together as a symbol of the magic which now ties the two of you together. I tie you together in love. I tie you together in life. I tie you together for as long as you both shall love.

Priest/ess 1 and 2 pick up the crowns of flowers. They place a crown on each handfaster's head.

Priest/ess 2: Oh, Mother of us all, You who have been with us always, You who have taught us the value of love, You who have shown us the value of kindness and the delight of passion, witness and seal the union of these two. With the magic of this circle, tie this couple together to share their lives.

Priest/ess 1: Father God, You who bring the strength of the forest, you who have shown us how to end and begin again, you who have manifested for us the power of spirit, witness and seal the union of these two. With the magic of this circle, tie this couple together to share their lives.

Vows

Priest/ess 2 (to handfaster 1): *Please repeat after me. I take you into my heart and give you my hand. In the presence of the God and Goddess and this crowd assembled, I pledge to you my love.*

Handfaster 1 repeats the words and puts the ring on handfaster 2's hand.

Priest/ess 1: (to handfaster 2) *I take you into my heart and give you my hand. In the presence of God and Goddess and this crowd assembled, I pledge to you my love.*

Handfaster 2 repeats the words and puts the ring on handfaster 1's hand.

Jumping the Broom

The broom is brought by the Maiden and held at a comfortable height in front of the couple. The handfasting couple holds hands and jumps over the broom.

Priest/ess 1 picks up cake and hands it to handfaster 2. Handfaster 2 turns toward handfaster 1.

Handfaster 2: May you never hunger for love, but always know it as a part of this relationship.

Priest/ess 2 hands cake to Handfaster 1. Handfaster 1 turns toward handfaster 2.

Handfaster 1: May you never hunger for love, but always know it as a part of this relationship.

Handfaster 1 feeds cake to handfaster 2. Priest/ess 2 hands the chalice to handfaster 1. Handfaster 1 turns toward handfaster 2.

Handfaster 1: May you never thirst for fulfillment, but always know it as a part of this relationship.

Handfaster 1 hands the chalice to handfaster 2.

Handfaster 2: May you never thirst for fulfillment, but always know it as a part of this relationship.

Handfaster 2 hands the chalice to Priest/ess 1, who returns it to the altar.

Priest/ess 2: By the powers of the Goddess, by the strength of the God, with the assistance of this company assembled and by the will of these two people, let it be known that (name) and (name) have been joined together. May their union be blessed always.

All: So mote it be!

Recessional music begins. The handfasted couple is led from the circle, followed by their attendants.

Appendix B:
Potential Timeline

Note: The statements in **bold** in this timeline are required activities. The *italicized* activities are optional. The sections in standard text refer to the reception.

First Steps

◆ **Pick the date of your handfasting.**

◆ **Discuss a budget, size and style of handfasting with your future partner and any others involved.**

◆ **Decide where your handfasting will be and, if necessary, reserve the place.**

◆ **Decide who will Priest/ess your handfasting and contact her/him to reserve the date.**

◆ **Find out if s/he requires an interview or counseling before performing a handfasting, and make arrangements if s/he does.**

◆ **Decide if you will have a reception and think in broad terms about how you want it to be.**

Six Months Before

◆ **Make a list of guests.**

◆ *Select attendants*

◆ *Choose clothing that the handfasters and attendants will wear, and order it if necessary.*

◆ *Make appointments for hair cut/styling, skin care, make-up, nails, and so forth.*

◆ *Make arrangements for music at the handfasting and/or reception.*

◆ *Decide on your decorations and find out where you can acquire them. If using a rental service, reserve needed items.*

◆ *Decide if you want to have photographs and make arrangements. If hiring a professional photographer, review samples of work and reserve the date with the photographer you choose.*

◆ Check out bakers if you want a cake.

Four Months Before

◆ **Complete your guest list.**

◆ *Order invitations.*

◆ *Order/find/collect decorations for handfasting and/or reception.*

◆ **Make arrangements to get to and from the handfasting** and from the reception to your honeymoon or home.

Three Months Before

◆ **Reserve a date with Priest/ess, the space and others involved to rehearse the ritual.**

◆ *Select and order rings.*

◆ *Make arrangements for travel after the handfasting.*

Two Months Before

◆ *Mail invitations.*

◆ *Each partner selects gifts for their partner and attendants.*

◆ *Make arrangements for out-of-town guest accommodations.*

◆ *Make arrangements for legal credentials.* **(Note: This is required for couples who want a marriage license.)**

One Month Before

◆ Have a final fitting of handfasting clothes.

◆ Finalize plans for the rehearsal *(and dinner)*.

◆ Inform all participants of the time, date and place of rehearsal.

◆ *Develop a plan for decorating the space for the handfasting and the reception.*

◆ *Designate someone to be in charge of decorating.*

◆ Make sure attendants have their clothes ready.

◆ *Check with newspapers on requirements for announcements.*

Two Weeks Before

◆ Do a final check with all the people who will participate.

◆ *Finalize transportation arrangements to and from handfasting, and from the reception to your honeymoon or home.*

◆ *Get the marriage license or domestic partnership registration (timing depends on the legal requirements in your state).* (Required for couples who want state recognition of their union.)

◆ *Visit the space where you and your attendants will change clothes for the handfasting and determine if it is adequate.*

◆ *Confirm arrangements with service providers involved in the ceremony and/or reception* (caterer, photographer, musicians/singers and florist).

One Week Before

◆ Review final details with those participating in the ritual.

◆ Appoint someone to handle any last-minute problems.

◆ *Pack for honeymoon travel and plan what you will wear after the reception.*

◆ Give final guest list/count to caterer.

One Day Before

◆ Give rings and Priest/esses fees to appropriate persons.

◆ Attend the rehearsal (and dinner).

◆ **At the rehearsal, the Priest/ess outlines the ritual for participants, and participants walk through their parts.**

Appendix C:
Budget / Finances

	Estimated	Actual
Ceremony		
Canopy	_____	_____
Flowers	_____	_____
Gowns/Accessories	_____	_____
Hair/Make-up	_____	_____
Headpiece/Veil	_____	_____
Legal credentials	_____	_____
Lighting	_____	_____
Musicians	_____	_____
Other decorations	_____	_____
Photography	_____	_____
Priest/ess	_____	_____
Rental equipment	_____	_____
Ring/s	_____	_____
Site	_____	_____
Tuxedo/es	_____	_____
Videotaping	_____	_____

	Estimated	Actual
Reception		
Cake	_____	_____
Catering	_____	_____
Decorations	_____	_____
Entertainment	_____	_____
Hall	_____	_____
Flowers	_____	_____
Photography	_____	_____
Rental equipment	_____	_____
Other		
Gifts for attendants	_____	_____
Rehearsal dinner	_____	_____
Thank-you cards	_____	_____
Transportation	_____	_____
Other	_____	_____

Appendix D:
Who Traditionally Pays for What

There are many ways to arrange the financial responsibilities involved in a handfasting. Due to the high cost of weddings, experts report that the current trend is toward more shared expenses between families. Plus, the average age of marrying couples is increasing, which means that more couples are financially self-sufficient and may pay many of their own wedding/handfasting expenses. (In 1990, the average age of a woman being married for the first time was 24; in 1950, the average age of a first-time bride was 18. The average age of men being married has risen as well.) In the increasing number of second marriages, many couples pay their own handfasting expenses as well.

Attendants usually pay for their own clothing, but either handfaster can offer to pay for all or part of an attendant's clothing. Following is the conventional division of expenses. But as always, it is your handfasting, and the first rule is to do what works best for you.

Bride's Parents

◆ Invitations and announcements
◆ Photography/videography
◆ The bride's trousseau
◆ The household trousseau
◆ All the cost of the reception
◆ The groom's ring
◆ Flowers for ceremony and reception
◆ Aisle runners, decorations and other appointments

◆ Custodian's fee, organist's fee, choir/musician fee

◆ A gift of substance for the couple

◆ Transportation for the bridal party

◆ The bride's dress

◆ Music at the ceremony and the reception

◆ Hotel expenses for out-of-town attendants, unless housed otherwise

◆ Flowers for the bride, her mother, father, grandmothers and attendants, and a boutonniere for her father

Groom's Parents

◆ The bride's ring

◆ The marriage license

◆ The bride's flowers

◆ The Priest/ess's fee

◆ The usher's gloves, ties and collars

◆ Gifts for the ushers

◆ Boutonnieres for the groom, the ushers and the groom's father

◆ Corsages for his mother and grandmothers

◆ A gift for the bride (usually jewelry)

◆ The honeymoon

◆ His handfasting/reception clothes and clothes for the honeymoon

◆ Hotel expenses for out-of-town ushers, unless housed otherwise

Appendix E:
A Checklist

Rehearsal (Dinner)
❑ Make a plan for everyone involved in the ceremony to rehearse the ritual.
❑ Reserve the place for the rehearsal.
❑ Finalize plans for rehearsal.
❑ Make reservations or otherwise arrange for the rehearsal dinner.
❑ Invite guests to the rehearsal dinner.
❑ Inform all participants of the time, date, and place of rehearsal.
❑ Attend the rehearsal.
❑ Priest/ess outlines ritual and participants walk through their parts.

Handfasting
❑ Pick a date.
❑ Discuss the budget, size and style of handfasting with your future partner and any others involved.
❑ If necessary, interview available Priest/esses and choose the one(s) you want to perform your ceremony.
❑ Find out if s/he requires an interview or counseling before per forming a handfasting and make arrangements.
❑ Select a place and reserve it.
❑ Reserve the place you selected.
❑ Make a guest list.
❑ Make arrangements for music.
❑ Select attendants.
❑ Order invitations.
❑ Mail invitations.

❑ Select and order rings.
❑ Select and order clothing.
❑ Try on the clothes you plan to wear.
❑ Visit the space where you and your attendants will change
       clothes and determine if it is adequate.
❑ Make sure attendants have their clothes ready.
❑ Decide what type of decorations you want.
❑ Order/find/collect decorations for handfasting.
❑ Make a plan for decorating the space and designate someone to
       be in charge.
❑ Decide if/how you want to have your handfasting/reception pho
tographed.
❑ Make arrangements with photographer.
❑ Make arrangements to get to and from the handfasting.
❑ If you are heterosexual or gay/lesbian in select locations and
       want to get a marriage license, find out the requirements.
❑ Get legal credentials.
❑ Do a final check of all the people who will participate.
❑ Give rings and Priest/esses fees to the appropriate person.
❑ Appoint someone to handle any last-minute problems.

Reception
❑ Decide if you will have a reception.
❑ Select a place.
❑ Reserve the place.
❑ Make arrangements for music.
❑ Sample/interview bakers.
❑ Decide what type of decorations you want.
❑ Order/find/collect decorations.
❑ Make a plan for decorating the space and designate someone to
       be in charge.

❑ Make plans to get to the reception and from there to your honeymoon or home.

❑ Try on what you plan to wear.

❑ Check with any service providers for the reception (caterer, florist, etc.).

❑ Give final guest list/count to caterer.

❑ Appoint someone to handle last-minute problems.

Other

❑ Make appointments for hair cut/styling, skin care, make-up, nails, and so forth.

❑ Arrange for travel after the handfasting.

❑ Select and purchase gifts for your partner and attendants.

❑ Arrange for out-of-town guest accommodations.

❑ Check with newspapers on requirements for handfasting announcements.

❑ Send announcement to newspapers.

❑ Pack for travel after handfasting and decide what you will wear to the reception.

Appendix F:
Legal Credentials

Marriage License

In most cases, your Priest/ess signs the marriage certificate. Be sure to check with the Priest/ess you have chosen to make certain s/he has the necessary credentials to officiate legally. Each state has different requirements. You may still have a Priest/ess who does not have legal credentials perform your ritual. S/he can perform your spiritual ceremony and a legally recognized official can marry you at another time. Names of civil officials available to perform these ceremonies are generally accessible through your county clerk's office or the local equivalent.

If you are a heterosexual couple or a lesbian/gay couple in select locations, it is up to you and your future partner to get the marriage license and comply with the legal and medical requirements of your state. This is usually done through your county court system* and requires a fee. Your application should be made in the county where the ceremony will take place. Check to see how long before the ceremony you must apply (it may be 30 days, or more or less). Some states require blood tests and a physical examination as part of the license application procedure. Most license fees need to be paid in cash and are not refundable. Generally, a license is valid for 30 days from the date it is issued.

If you are being handfasted to a person of the same sex and are not in an area where you can get a marriage license, you may be able to register your domestic partnership. If you do not know whether your area recognizes same-sex marriages or partnerships, check with a local lesbian- or gay-rights organization or the National Gay and Lesbian Task Force, 1700 Kalorama Rd., Washington, DC 20009; 202.332.6483; www.ngltf.org.

What to Take Along When You Apply for a License

Check with the office in your area that issues marriage licenses or domestic partnerships to see what documentation you need to take with you. The documentation typically required includes:

◆ A form of identification which shows your address.

◆ A certified copy of your birth certificates. Certified copies bear an embossed seal, date and the signature of the State Registrar* or Register of Deeds.* The seal of a notary public is not accepted for certification of a vital record. Photocopies are not accepted nor are uncertified hospital records. A birth certificate may be purchased at the Register of Deeds Office* or State Vital Records Office where you were born.

◆ If you have been married before, you will need a certified copy of your divorce decree or annulment from your most recent marriage. (In most states, divorced persons may not remarry until 6 months after the divorce judgment. Check with local officials to see what the laws are where you plan to marry.)

◆ If you are under 18, check on your state's requirements. In many states, people under 18 can marry with the signed consent of their parents. Consent forms may be available at the County Clerk's* office.

You also need to know:

◆ The name of the city, village, or township and county where you currently live

◆ The correct spelling of both parents of both individuals (first, middle and last, including mothers' maiden names)

◆ The date and place where your handfasting will take place
◆ The name of your Priest/ess

*Or the equivalent in your area

Appendix G:
Creating Vows

There is no right or wrong way to compose vows. You may already know the perfect poem, song or verse that symbolizes your bond, and such selection(s) can easily be incorporated into your vows. Another option is to check the dictionary or a thesaurus for words which you associate with handfastings. You can read dictionary definitions as given or elaborate on a word's meaning in your own way.

Inspiring vows can be made by creating statements about how you felt about your partner when you first knew her/him, how you feel about him/her now and how you anticipate feeling in the future. For more ideas, review the options below.

◆ What do you think is the nature of love?

◆ How did you feel the first time you met/saw your partner?

◆ What was the first thing you observed about your partner?

◆ What do you think creates a family?

◆ What is the nature of the bond you and your partner share?

◆ How do you envision the future with your partner?

◆ What do you believe is the essence of partnership?

◆ How do you feel about making a commitment to another person?

◆ What interests do you and your partner have in common?

◆ Was there a single event that was an important turning point in your relationship?

◆ Do you and your partner share a spiritual tradition? How does this affect your partnership?

◆ What do you believe your life will be like as you age with your partner?

◆ How do you envision daily life with your partner?

Index